FOR THE PRESENT

poetry *Pt* today

FOR THE PRESENT

Edited by
Julie Bomber

First published in Great Britain in 1997 by Poetry Today, an imprint of Penhaligon Page Ltd, Upper Dee Mill, Llangollen, Wales.

A Catalogue record for this book is available from the British Library.

ISBN 1862260079

Typesetting and layout, Penhaligon Page Ltd, Wales.
Printed and bound by Forward Press Ltd, England

'Time present and time past
Are both perhaps present in time future,
And time future contained in time past.

T S Eliot (1888-1965)

SERIES INTRODUCTION

The Poetry Today series of anthologies was launched to provide a substantial showcase for today's poets. A permanent record of perception, concern and creativity in our late twentieth century lives.

Poetry is a coat of many colours. Today's poets write in a limitless array of styles: traditional rhyming poetry is as alive and kicking today as modern free-verse. Language ranges from easily accessible to intricate and elusive.

Poems have a lot to offer in our fast-paced 'instant' world. Reading poems gives us an opportunity to sit back and explore ourselves and the world around us.

Today's poetry readers have as varied tastes as the poets who write for them. The poems in this volume complement each other and provide insight into the real life of a society heading for the third millennium.

FOREWORD

For the Present captures the mood of our times. This anthology, the fourth in the series, presents a multi-faceted viewpoint of the human experience.

The Poets, come together in this volume to reflect on universal emotions such as, love and hate, friendship, despair and passion. Subjects range from intimate looks at life on a personal level, to comments on a broader scale about the state of society.

I have enjoyed compiling *For the Present*, I hope you will share the poet's thoughts, feelings, experience some of their emotion and stop to ponder the nature of life - *for the present.*

Contents

The Poems

Notes

Written as a solo, for per-
formance by bass or tenor,
this poem, together with sev-
eral others, has been set to
music by the author, an erst-
while piano teacher and mu-
sic specialist in junior schools.
Many of these Christmas
songs and carols were per-
formed by children in her
classes, at concerts and music
festivals.

Inspiration for writing these
poems is based on her experi-
ence of the interests and re-
sponses of the children to the
work she presents. She also
writes for adult groups. She is
greatly influenced by nature
in all its forms and moods.
Her favourite poets are Keats
and Wordsworth; she also
directs performances of
Shakespeare's plays (for
which she writes the music to
the songs).

The Shepherd to his Grandson

A lonely life, we tended sheep,
The little town lay wrapped in sleep,
The wolves drew near around the fold,
We shivered in the freezing cold.
The sheep looked up in sudden fear -
It was the turning of the year.

Suddenly, we saw a star,
An angel's voice called from afar,
There Gabriel stood in golden light,
The wolves fled howling in the night.
We shepherds trembled at the sight,
It was the turning of the year.

'Shepherds, seek the Babe that is born
Find God's Son in stable forlorn.'
Hurrying there on that wonderful night,
We found the sweet Babe in dim candlelight,
We found the three kings, and Mary so fair,
The oxen, and Joseph who welcomed us there -
It was the turning of the year.

And sometimes now, on quiet days,
Tending my sheep in summer haze,
The picture in my mind still clear
My thoughts return to that Babe so dear,
Sent from Heaven to all people here -
It was the turning of the year.

Beryl Louise Penny

Notes

Josephine Haden lives near Harrogate; she is married and has no children.

Her writing has included articles, short stories, comic verse for family occasions, nativity plays (some in verse), carols and hymns (with music). Whilst a member of the local Writers' Circle, some years ago, prizes were won.

Her interests are reading, music, tapestry, travel, wildlife, the countryside and calligraphy.

Most ideas for poetry arrive in the middle of a sleepless night! A single phrase will develop into a complete poem almost immediately, needing only 'tidying up' and minor re-phrasing the following morning.

A vapour trail in the sky resulted in *The Jet*.

The Jet

Day flight

The pencil streak of white quickly appears,
spreading across the blue backcloth of sky,
widening into bands of clouds. One hears
no sound from those heights of infinity.
Yet with painstaking searching one might trace
a flash of silver, like a shooting star
(there!) hurtling through the endless void of space -
the jet 'plane, streaking down toward the far
horizon (lying as a taut black line
in distant east). And wheeling down the arc
of sky, the high-pitched screaming of engines
assails the ears with unexpected shock.

Night flight

The giant monster speeds to dark from light.
The earth is black, but clustering lights abound
(like heaven upside down!). And through the night
it seeks its haven on the jewelled ground,
dips to pursue the black-frosted runway,
and noses down the corridor to glide
between the glowing lights that keep at bay
curtains of darkness hanging on each side.

Josephine Haden

Notes

I am 57 years of age and married. I'm a classical music enthusiast, composing and playing light music.

I started writing poetry recently, when I became more aware of the problems of the third world and its people. This poem was inspired by the general abuse of the countryside and man's attempts to upset nature.

The poem is dedicated to my daughter, Andrea.

Nature's Window

As I gaze out through my window,
I feel humble and so small.
Looking out onto nature,
and the reality of it all.

When I look across the meadow,
I see flowers of every hue.
Sweet grass of crushed velvet,
the dampness of the morning dew.

On gazing into an icy stream,
dazzled by its shimmering mirror,
its reflection seems to beckon me,
to come a little nearer.

I look deep into the forest,
trees so silent, yet so tall,
branches reach out, as though to touch me,
I feel safe, no fear at all.

As I look towards snow-capped mountains,
so imposing, in the morning sky.
Wild heather, and majestic pines,
a shroud of grey mist hangs high.

As I gaze through the window of the world,
no cracks and no flaws.
We must protect all beauty beyond,
and cherish the wonder of it all.

Wendy L Patrick

Notes

I am 62 years of age and have been writing verse on and off for the past 40 years.

My verse has been published in the Easterner, a local government quarterly magazine, over a period of 16 years. However, I only recently began entering competitions in 1995 and to date, six have been published by The International Library of Poetry.

All my work is based mainly on topical events, although this verse could have been written at any time during those 40 years.

English

Two young boys attended school,
One thought bright the other a fool.
The former had command of words,
And though it did appear absurd.
Apart from the way he spoke
His knowledge really was remote.

The latter boy was far from dim,
But words alas were strange to him.
He knew the meaning of what was said
And practically was far ahead.
But if you know just what to say,
With anything you get away!

English gets you into power,
Though others may above you tower.
That is why there's such a mess,
As knowledge some do not possess.
In fact, some are really dense!
Having no idea of common sense!

D R Thomas

Notes

I was born in Barking, Essex, 5th June 1977, and have one older sister, Sarah 20, and one younger, Lisa, 11. I have lived in Herne Bay, Kent, for six and a half years.

My inspiration comes from my life, friends and feelings. I am lucky enough to be able to put words to some of my feelings. I hope others can relate to these words.

Throughout my life I have had support, but none more than from my closest friends and fellow inspired Saul Bibby, Sarah Brown and Joel Dunn.

It is to them I dedicate this poem, and not forgetting Tiffany.

Deep Blue

I'd hit out if I knew who to hit
So I'll take this knife and sink it deep
And so this flesh that is so weak
Through beaded drops of red shall weep
And I with thee heaven-bound
Shall through these clouds
With exiled heart leap and sound
And you who had once known me
Shall no longer my face see

Hazel Aldridge

Notes

My name is Licia Carlotta Ottanelli-Johnston; I was born in Florence, Italy, on 5th June 1926. I was educated in Italy and came to England in 1951, training as a nurse in Surrey. I settled in Kent, marrying in 1957 and have one son and two granddaughters. I worked as a part-time nurse, mostly with children, and recently retired.

I have been writing poetry since my early teens; thirty years ago, after I obtained O level English Literature, I started again, writing poems and short stories.

During 1994/96, I have had ten poems published by Arrival Press and Triumph House of Peterborough, in various anthologies.

I am influenced by Browning and Wordsworth. I like to write about nature and mankind. This poem was inspired by memories of my Italian childhood.

Childhood Summers

Under a cloudless sky,
we walked through the wood.
These were happy days,
the summers of my childhood.

In ripe golden meadows,
we ran after one another.
I remember being the shadow
of my clever, big brother.

Busy, free holiday time
spent fishing in little brooks,
with a string for a fishing line
and a sort of home-made hooks.

Summers of incandescent fireflies,
chasing for endless hours,
bright coloured butterflies
flitting from flower to flower.

Yearly, we left the city bustle
for the Tirrenian seaside.
Building tunnels and sand castles,
waiting for the incoming tide.

Weekend family outing
to the park of the Cascine,
flying the kite, shouting
or splashing in the piscine.

Under the blazing sun,
we went picking blackberry.
Blessed, innocent fun,
we were young and merry.

Licia C Johnston

Notes

Born in 1955, in Boldon Colliery, County Durham, a small north east village between Newcastle and Sunderland; I have lived and taught in Wakefield, West Yorkshire, since 1978.

The Invigilator is written from the point of view of the teacher who remembers, only too well, the trauma of sitting exams. Invigilators feel a great empathy with the students, and frustration at being unable to render assistance, as in the normal teaching situation. They must remain incapacitated; silent observing constables of the examination institution.

Dedicated to teachers and students the world over on the great search for knowledge and self-fulfilment.

The Invigilator

I sit here in silence, complete, watching them,
sitting in rows for their final exam,
but at least they've got something to do in this void,
where as I may just sit here and feel paranoid,
thinking 'This job could be done by a well-trained android';
and the time passes on ever slowly.

It's like watching paint dry, or a World War Two torture,
being on madness' edge, a kind of brain slaughter.
Some have stopped working but some still work on,
the feeling in fingers now long since has gone.
Will they ever escape from this dire marathon?
And the time passes on ever slowly.

I'm falling asleep with the tedium,
slipping down in my seat with delirium.
I wish I was somewhere else other than here,
where behaviour is normal and thinking is clear,
perhaps sat in a pub with a cool glass of beer;
and the time passes on ever slowly.

A voice calls out 'You've got ten minutes left!'
Expressions suggest that there has been a theft.
Short hairs on their necks stand up prickly.
Some still writing, so frantic, so quickly.
The looks on some faces quite sickly;
and no longer is time passing slowly.

Some give furtive glances,
'How was it for the other's?'
In this shared experience
they are sisters and brothers.
Some feel 'What will be will be,
and hang the repercussions.'
The voice says 'Finish there please
and let's have no discussions.
Put your pens and pencils down,
then wait for your instructions';
and the time . . . once again . . . passes slowly.

Trevor Caine

Notes

I am 31 years old and have one brother. We are a close family and my parents are very supportive. My occupation is that of a nurse and I have worked for the past 14 years in the NHS. I have lived in Norfolk for six years and will soon be moving to North Lincolnshire in the new year.

This is my first poem to be published and I am in the process of researching for a novel (fantasy).

I started writing poetry at school and have a great fondness for Scotland very inspirational. I have a family history of Scottish descent.

This poem was written for and dedicated to Dave, my partner and best friend, with much love, always.

What it Takes

I'll walk in the shadows
If that's what it takes
For you to see me
I'll talk in whispers
If that's what it takes
For you to hear me
I'll lay alone most nights
If that's what it takes
For you to want me
I'll hang on every word
If that's what it takes
For you to tell me
Just wrap your soul around me
That's all that it takes
For me to love you
Tell me your dreams
That's all that it takes
For you to trust me

Della Roads

Eternal Flower
Memories of Grandma

Notes

I am 21 years old, studying English at Swansea University.

Other poems to be published soon: *Happiness (a Modern Disease)* and *Reality Within a Dream*.

I started writing poetry when I was about 15 years old and then moved on to short stories more recently.

I am inspired by a love for people and nature and a hope that one day my poetry might make people stop and think.

This poem is about Marjorie Minor, who passed away last June. She was loved and respected by all who met her for being full of happiness and having an exuberance for life, she, and others like her, will never be forgotten.

The flower which withers 'ere November,
Returns to its splendour in the month of June,
And though it lies in the ground, we remember
Like the melody of an angel's tune.

The presence of one so loved will never fade,
Now the physical to ashes has gone.
Leaving the impression happiness made,
Memories, like the soul in mind, live on.

Ben Brown

I am a Camera

I am the camera that never lies because I am the camera that never tries,
To do anything other than watch and observe. Look through my lens
                                at the voices unheard
And you too will see why the blurred edges grow; for what shall ye reap,
                                so then shall ye sow.

A snapshot of life is all I provide. A weed, a cloud, driftwood on the ebb tide,
A double exposure; that's how I sound, from the mix of the sky
                                to the roof on the ground.
Adjust my focus and it all becomes clear, except for the ones
                                now unwilling to hear.

'What good is sitting alone in your room? Come hear the music play!'
But I pull down the shutters, retreat to my womb and make sure
                                I have nothing to say.
My case heard in camera, my camera in case where the darkness
                                develops around.
A camera obscura in my latinate dark room, where still I exist
                                without sound.

I am a camera whose eyes see the light and the dark in equivalent measure.
I've a balance to strike. Do I talk when I like or just capture those
                                moments of pleasure?
Your enjoyment I steal, but like Faraday's wheel, my persistence
                                of vision remains.
When the Zoetrope spins and the laughter begins, from my life's panorama,
                                I abstain.

I am a camera whose pictures are framed by the gallery of false
                                understanding.
The pretensions of those who are quick to oppose my right to be heard, by
                                their deeds, are demanding
A silence of mind which I cannot allow. I am a camera whose villainy now
Would be to ignore all the sights I have seen; to refuse my place in the
                                Pharaoh's dream.

For though I may stutter or stumble and fall, I am a camera and I speak
        loudest of all.

Frank Geoghegan-Quinn

Notes

Now 21 years old, I am going through a difficult time; working towards a public career makes it even harder. I am 'gender disphoric', which means I was born into a male body but believe I should be physically female.

Being brought up as a male whilst living inside, both emotionally and mentally, as a female, is traumatic. Recently, I have begun to seek support and advice whilst I gain confidence.

I dedicate it to those like myself, their friends and family, and with my loving thanks to Stuart, David, Shelley, Rose and Graham.

Sandie

If one day you spoke to me
Whilst out shopping in the town
What would you see before you
As you look me up and down

Would I be a happy young lad
Who always helps out his friends
Someone who shows his feelings
And lovingly makes amends

Or would you see the showman
Who needs ambition and drive
A boy who wants to be seen
On the path where he can thrive

If society met me
Let's say twenty years ago
I would have been a misfit
A freak for a circus show

People then would not believe
That young men could feel this way
They would all shout 'I'm ill'
And give me treatment every day

The scientists and doctors
Would try to find me a cure
But the problem's source was vague
And everyone was unsure

Nowadays it's different
People appreciate more
What it is to be human
And it's not against the law

To show people how I feel
Express myself, not put to shame
The way I look, walk and talk
And why I want a girlie name

All I want in future
Is to be liked and told I can
I am that sweet girl you see
But Sandie was born a man!

Andriana Catherine Holloway

Unhappy House

Unhappy house of memories -
The motley disarray
Of rotting love that never died
And never went away -
Leaving just its quiet ghosts
Crouching in the hall,
Drifting through the empty rooms,
Touching every wall.
Unhappy house, where secrets live
Festering, congealed;
Heavy hearts still breaking -
Wounds that never healed.

Unhappy house, I think of you
All along the years;
I still run crying in my dreams
Back up familiar stairs,
To where your murmuring phantoms
Still tread the dusty floor,
Still watch behind the windows
Still wait behind the door
Patiently to take me
In their sorrowful caress,
To wrap their arms around my soul
With dreadful tenderness.

Vivienne Allen

Notes

I believe the most precious thing we have is the love of God. In writing verse I try to convey this message to any-one who has ears to hear.

My lifestyle is simple and as close to nature as I can get. I live in a rural setting and have dogs, cats, goats, hens, bees and a large vegetable garden.

Writing verse is a new and exciting experience enabling me to express my thoughts and feelings in a constructive way.

Grief

I will not grieve for you today.
I cannot.

Although our time has passed away
And I shall miss you more each day,
I sorrow not.

You will be with me everywhere
My time remaining you will share,
I know it.

And though you are not here with me
I am content as I can be,
I'll show it.

For you are with our Lord above
Secure and cherished by His love,
I know it.

And though my heart would have me sad
My spirit says I should be glad
And show it.

Enjoy the heavenly pastures bright,
That place above that needs no light.
Where glory reigns, there is no night to darken all,
Oh what a sight!

How can I sorrow then for you
Believing strongly as I do
There's such a place? For God is true
And cares for such as we, the two
Who will not mourn, each for the other,
But trust in God that we'll discover,
Believers all, sister and brother,
Will rest like you.

Do we believe?
Of course we do.

I will not grieve for you today.
I cannot.

Glenys Godfrey

Notes

I was born in Warwickshire, but now live in West Yorkshire with my husband and three sons.

Writing poetry has been a hobby of mine since childhood, but it was my impending fortieth birthday that prompted me to bring my poems out of the closet. Although this poem is most certainly about me, I believe that it will strike a chord with many housewives and mothers.

Another of my poems, *And She Waited . . .* has recently been accepted for publication by The International Library of Poetry.

Housewife's Dilemma

It seems I spend my life
Just making plans.
Quite simply, I'm a wife,
Not someone grand.

But as the years creep by
My yearnings grow.
Am I just scared to die
With naught to show?

I remember having dreams
When I was young,
But these turned into schemes
For having fun.

And now I think I need
To stake my claim.
To finally succeed,
Achieve some fame.

So here I sit and write
This simple rhyme,
Hoping that it might
Be worth my time.

I'll make one final plea,
Before I close.
Have sympathy for me
And read my prose.

Rossline O'Gara

I Know You Knew Me Too

The pain it is all over me
I am trying to stay calm,
But the fear is building up inside
There will be nothing in these arms.

I can't believe the words they say
But there's bloodstain in the bed,
My heart will beat out of my chest
There's a pounding in my head.

I saw your picture on the screen
I felt your every move,
I took the rest they told me to
And still your life I lose.

I had you there inside of me
I ate to make you strong,
And now I find for all I did
That you are really gone.

Your time it had not come yet
I haven't seen your face,
I lived on months of loving you
And for our first embrace.

There's family all around me now
But they feel so far away,
The darkness does surround me
I lost my life with you that day.

I know that you were really there
And I know you knew me too,
I talked to you and sang you songs
And you slept as I stroked you.

I pray wherever you may be
That you are safe and warm,
That danger knows not where you are
And you are far from harm.

My own child is no longer here
And I know not where you rest,
I can't even see you in my mind
Or hold you to my breast.

So goodnight my sleeping angel
One day I'll hold you tight,
When my life here is over
And I begin the endless night.

Callista Chambers

Notes

Antonia Connell now lives in Hampshire and has a special interest in gardening and ecology.

Antonia started writing in 1991 and draws inspiration from nature and the wider Gaia movement.

Freedom

A prison without a door or lock,
Holding captive its passive flock,
Longer than any with lock and key,
Causing no end of misery.
To be free at last from this strangling pain,
Is as soothing as softly falling rain.

Antonia Connell

Notes

I was born in Norwich in 1951 and spent most of my life in and around Norfolk. Although I now live in Australia, my heart will always belong in England. I am a sole parent of three girls and have raised them all on my own. At present, I work for Home-care and enjoy listening to wonderful stories from the elderly.

Most (not all) of my poems are inspired from actual events and always come straight from the heart.

My ambition is to write a poem equal to our great poets of the past.

The Fishermen

'Twas the calm before the storm
And the sea was as still as the night,
An eerie, ghostly feeling fell about
As the moon shone a glistening light.
Suddenly a breeze blew strongly from the north
And I could see a boat not far from the shore,
I could hear the waves pounding the rocks below
As the breeze blew into a mighty roar.
I screwed up my face in disbelief
I couldn't believe what was happening before my eyes
I wanted to get help yet I wanted to run
But all I could hear were the men and their cries.
The boat was being tossed ever-higher ever-lower
As the waves crashed onto its hull
I could hear the crew yelling as the rain came down
Then the yelling transformed into a lull.
The boat disappeared into the depth of the sea
And the crew had vanished from my sight,
Only I would ever know as I stood soaked to the skin
About the storm, the fishermen and their plight.

Amanda Taunton

Notes

I'm 40, married, living in Halifax, but was born and raised in the Potteries.

Forward Press and Anchor Books have published eight of my poems in anthologies, and Threads magazine is to publish my first short story in 1997.

I'm self-publishing Snapshots, a collection of my poems; £2 each and 50p per copy sold goes to Mencap. Anyone interested?

Finally, why I wrote *Street Piper*. Two years ago I saw a young lass sitting in a Basingstoke subway. This poem is for her and about her; my message is that our children deserve better than this.

Street Piper

Penny-whistler
play merry tunes
welcome autumn's amber hues
swirling by
on the other side

Your thin face
and gaunt frame
beg for loose change
child, why are you here?

If winter comes
without a home
will you haunt our streets
the way your empty eyes haunt me?

Paul L Birkin

If

If I was a camel
I'd have a big hump,
And if I was a rabbit
I'd jump, jump, jump.

If I was a lion
I'd live in a zoo,
And if I was a silly cow
I'd moo, moo, moo.

If I was a unicorn
I'd have a horn in front,
And if I was a big fat pig
I'd grunt, grunt, grunt.

If I had a name like *Jaws*
I'd probably be a shark,
And if I was a naughty dog
I'd bark, bark, bark.

If I was a ghost
With a white robe on,
I wouldn't hang about
I'd be gone, gone, gone.

Jeff Simon

Notes

I'm a 25 year old who is training as an actor in London, after taking the trip of my life through Europe by train.

This poem came to fruition during seven hours in a train station at Bordeaux. I had arrived that morning with my travelling partner and, after a few hours investigating the town, we decided to find greener pastures. Armed with the only English newspaper we could find, we decided to sit and wait for our overnight train, rather than face the unpleasant environment outside. This poem was a view through my eyes during those hours.

Bordeaux

Smelly, dirty, rude.
Train station like a brothel
Shouting men with naked tops
Unsightly streets
Rubbish everywhere
Is this Bordeaux?

Foreign men eyeing bags
Ready to pickpocket
Pretending to limp
Drinking from unmarked bottles
Talking in slurs
Sleeping like a coma

Watch our bags
Keep our guard up
Trust no one
Hate Bordeaux
Glad to be leaving
The dirtiness seeps into our pores
If we leave, will this dirt leave us?

B Chapman

Unspoken Love

Notes

This poem is about a person, who is too shy to let the person they like know, as I used to be.

Won't you tell me what to do?
I've been silly enough to fall for you.
I haven't told you how I feel,
My thoughts of you I can't reveal.

Though I see you every day,
I never know just what to say.
To talk to you, I know I ought,
But I also know, it can come to nought.

I wish that I, could let you know,
Just how much I love you so.
I wish I could tell you, of my plight,
I even dream of you at night.

Even though, you are available,
I still find myself unable,
To tell you, what is in my heart,
I can never send you Cupid's dart.

A Derbyshire

Notes

A serious accident in his teens left Keith Browne with severe head injuries and impaired learning ability. Over years of poor health, he has struggled with his education and, through evening class and day release courses, achieved the necessary passes, at both ordinary and advanced level, to enter Bath College of Higher Education in 1965, to gain, after three years, a Certificate in Education.

After teaching science for some years at secondary schools in the West of England, he returned to Bath College of Higher Education in a supportive role, being particularly interested in Post Graduate studies. He was one of a team who supported science courses at the college. Taking early retirement in 1996, he is able to devote his time to creative writing.

Unconditionally Broken describes a young woman's influence on an elderly recluse, who is as mesmerised by her youth and vitality as she is by his isolation. Introduced to her world of bars and parties, she leaves his life as quickly as she entered it. *Unconditionally Broken* sums up and expresses the man's feelings of both gain and his subsequent sense of loss, on her departure.

Unconditionally Broken

A brightness, born of living,
Took his hand
And joy became his youth.

The dreams, undreamed, were met
The hopes, unmet, fulfilled.

Now shadows cast remain
Which once her radiance
Would dispel.

And sadness fills the lonely eyes
That sparkled once
When brightness held his hand.

Keith Browne

Notes

The author is sixty years old, married thirty one years, with two grown up children and three young grandchildren, did national service in the army, is a machinist and lives in the West Midlands. Has penned a few verses, most of which were written whilst laid up after an accident, about twenty years ago. Likes making models, musical boxes, etc and photography.

Reverie

Memories are like a breath of the past,
A whisper to the mind, let it last,
Summer morning mists, soft and grey,
Blocking reality, clouding the way.

To lapse into pleasantries from long ago,
Is a freedom of mine, to escape from a foe,
My foe is common to all of mankind,
Boredom, through labour, is a danger I find

But when I'm alone, and left to my thoughts,
There is no danger of being distraught,
For 'tis then my mind wanders, Utopia-bound,
Rustling leaves, and singing birds, the only sounds,
A soul at peace is everyone's dream.

J W Clark

Notes

I am 34, married with one child. I'm a chemical engineer, working for a large multi-national chemical company. I live close to Londonderry, Northern Ireland.

I have had only a few poems published before. I have written many based on the 'troubles' in Northern Ireland, the subject which has inspired most of my work. I have been writing poetry most of my life, which is ironic since I was terrible at English language and literature at school.

I enjoy sightseeing with my family and I am a fanatic of the X Files and Father Ted.

The Summer of Dreams is about the experiences I had when I spent a summer (1982) in Dublin. I was a student at Queen's University, Belfast. The summer was an escape from the stresses I felt in my life at that time. The poem was written to a person whom I met and worked with during the summer, selling copies of ink drawings to tourists. He became a close friend and we've been friends ever since. That summer was special.

The Summer of Dreams

I wish I was back,
To that summer a few years ago,
To be with the people as I knew them then,
When time went so slow.
Days on the street,
Selling our lines and buying a laugh,
We had a hell of a time
And a half.
The sun always shone,
And we made enough to get by,
So we'd lie on our backs and soak it all up,
And stare at our limit the sky.
We would talk,
We shared a lifetime in weeks,
The valleys were low,
But we climbed to the top of our peaks.
And the city would open its hand,
So we could walk down its roads,
Spilling the banter like sawdust,
And sharing our loads.
And at night,
We'd go out at the end of our day,
See a film, have a packet of chips and a bun,
And blow all our pay.
But who cares, it was class,
Each week would give us new sight,
But the end of the heat of the summer
Approached like the night . . .

. . . These days I go back on the train now and then,
I still keep in touch with a few.
The years cannot darken the memories,
That are ever-new.
But I wish I was back,
What I'd give to go through it again,
My summer of dreams lives forever,
As alive now as it was then.

Stuart Grant

A Dream About My Children's Room

In the silence of the night, I think I dreamed a dream,
I thought I heard my children, in their bedroom so it seemed.
I'm sure I heard their giggles, and talking in their sleep,
So I thought it best that I should rise, and take a tiny peep.

I tip-toed on the landing top, as quiet as could be,
And wondered at this time of night, what picture I would see.
But alas when I looked in their room, I saw no tiny heads,
The covers were all neatly drawn. No one was in their beds.

I realised then how years had passed, from children they had grown,
And like the little birds outside, they from their nest had flown.
A vision then appeared to me, I saw they were all well,
Tucked in their cosy homes afar, no need to toll the bell.

I stood and looked a moment there, into the empty room,
And felt a little sad at heart, and just a little gloom.
An inner voice then said to me, 'Their lives are in full stream,'
And I should go to bed again, perhaps I only dreamed a dream.

Donald Futer

The Dream

Notes

I am 77 years of age and live in one of the villages of the Suffolk Heritage coastal area, near to the RSPB bird reserve at Minsmere.

The poem was based on an actual dream.

I wish to dedicate my poem to my life-long friend, Gwen Maddison.

One day I fell asleep and dreamed I was a bird
And as I glided through the air
I knew just how a bird must feel,
And felt a joy most rare.
Elation filled my body, my heart near burst with joy
For I had known in that short time a thrill beyond compare.
The dream was over all too soon, I wakened with a sigh
My mind returned to consciousness, the sun by now was high.
Ne'er would I forget the dream until the day I die,
Maybe then perhaps I'd be a bird up in the sky.

Violet E Harvey

Loss

Notes

I am a widow, a retired teacher (previously a journalist) and have always written both poetry and prose. Recently, I have sold verses to a well-known card manufacturer, and enjoyed this limited challenge.

Bereavement lasts a long time.
It takes some understanding.
Those who think it's lost its sting
Are wrong. They don't know a thing,
For suddenly it hits you.
Your loved one isn't coming back.
No matter how you may pretend,
It is a fact - no doubt about it.
He isn't coming back.
So how can we live on, bereft,
Legless, hugless?

We know we have to journey on
Somehow, somewhere, some way.
Bereavement lasts a long time.
It never goes.
It only fades with time.

P M Jay

Noel

November's grey and cloudy days are done,
The mists and tints of autumn long since gone,
The leafless trees stand gaunt against the sky,
The short dark days of winter looming nigh.

But then to cast the cloak of gloom away
The Advent and the joys of Christmas Day,
The time for love, and grateful hearts to fill
With generous thoughts, forgiveness and goodwill.

With praise and thanks we shed a humble tear
For blessings granted through the passing year,
Mindful of those afflicted and in need,
We pray that from their troubles they'll be freed,

The old year gaily dies and with the morn
Are hopeful expectations newly born,
Fresh promises and vows to mend our ways,
What matter if they only last for days?

Reginald E Miles

Notes

I was born and bred in London and am now an elderly person. I moved to Worthing eleven years ago, but always regard myself as a Londoner.

Over the years I have written a large amount of poems, many of which were read out on the LBC Nightline programme, Poets' Corner. I was runner-up in the Queen's Silver Jubilee competition, and have had numerous poems in magazines.

The Lottery

It isn't right - it can't be right
So all the critics say
For folk to spend their hard-earned cash
The lottery to play.

The most they can expect to win
Is just a ten-pound share.
It's only one in millions
Who becomes a millionaire.

It isn't wrong, it can't be wrong
We hear the gamblers utter
To spend a pound or two each week
To have a little flutter.

A small amount won't break us
Just think what we could buy.
A Rolls, a yacht, a mansion.
And it's so worthwhile to try.

But would they give to charity
Or people in distress
Or hand some of their winnings
To the hard-up NHS?

Well yes - I think that some might
For not everyone is greedy.
And there are some who'd find delight
In sharing with the needy.

Celia White

49

Notes

I have been writing ditties since I was at school. I have written poetry for a number of years, had some of my poems published, and several of them broadcast on BBC Radio, but have not yet reached the pinnacle of fame! My satisfaction is achieved merely by writing what I cannot communicate to people in general.

I am now a grandmother; I have reared four children who are now all very independent and living their own separate lives. I love my family dearly and write mostly about children, people - not material issues (though I can) and I have a special need to communicate.

I was inspired to write *Our Mother Tongue* because of my abhorrence of the way English is presented in all its forms in this day and age: television, radio, national newspapers etc. I become so incensed by the way people, especially children, speak nowadays. None of us is perfect but we can all try to achieve perfection in all our ways.

I enjoy music, crosswords, quiz programmes, philately and gardening; I have a great affinity with Mother Earth and I love my garden.

Thomas de Quincey - 1785-1859.

Our Mother Tongue

Whatever happened to English? The language we were taught.
The grammar and the spelling now seem to count as nought.
We were always told, when you write a composition,
Don't ever start a sentence with a preposition.

Now, it doesn't seem to matter where you put your *and* and *but*,
They all fit together, we're in a dreadful rut.
What happened to King's English? That's what it once was called.
If past masters could hear it, I'm sure they'd be appalled.

I talk to present teachers, they don't seem to care,
So long as one can understand the words as written there.
Words once had a meaning, and a special function.
To join two phrases together, one needed a conjunction.

I read the daily papers and listen to the news,
To understand good English, computers are no use.
Then there is the infinitive which so often must be split.
Oh! This imperfect English makes me want to spit.

So what! You might say, what is imperfection?
Does it really matter? So we accept rejection.
And now I quote a master, Thomas de Quincey,
I can't recall the date. He said;
'Even imperfection can have its ideal or perfect state.'

Joanne Quinton

Notes

I am a 17 year old student at Windsor School, a Service Children's school in Germany, studying my first year of A level English Literature. I have written very little poetry to date, and *Some People* is my first attempt at a Shakespearean style sonnet. I prefer to spend my time writing songs, for the band in which I play (called 'Binary'), and short stories for friends to read.

In my spare time I play football for a local German team, and enjoy playing guitar. In the future I hope to go on to university and eventually work in the leisure industry.

Some People

Some people think when you cry you're sad
They give you space and hope you'll sort it out
There is a time for crying when you're mad
You want to fight and even scream and shout
Some people think that when you run you're scared
Life's got so bad you feel you have to leave
When a problem's solved a problem is shared
Speak to your friends and they'll help you believe
Some people think when you laugh you've had fun
A joke's been told or an error's been made
Don't dwell on the past what's done has been done
If others mock you don't run for the shade
      Life takes turns for the good and for the bad
      Believe in yourself and you won't feel sad.

Neil Harmsworth

Notes

I am 75 years old and retired, obviously. I was born in Leeds, Yorkshire, but now live with my wife here, in Bishop Auckland, County Durham.

For some time I have painted (water colour) as a hobby but decided, about three months ago, to try my hand at poetry. My first poem was a simple religious one, inspired after watching a church service on television. I have now written about twenty five poems, on various themes which seem to just come to mind.

Autumn was because I actually looked out of the window one morning and realised that autumn was nigh, and the rest came naturally.

Autumn

When I looked out this morning,
Autumn, I knew, was nigh.
The mist the hills adorning,
The racing clouds on high.

The dappled orange patches,
On sycamore and oak,
The way the wind despatches,
The cottage chimney's smoke.

The hips and haws in hedgerows,
The chestnut's spiky fruit.
The now redundant scarecrows,
Migrating birds en route.

The stubble in the wheat-field,
The endless bales of hay.
Now that harvest bells have peeled,
Shows summer's had its day.

The rowan's ripe red berries,
The fern and bracken brown,
Children's cheeks like cherries,
The odd leaf falling down.

The whole world needs a resting time,
Let nature fallow lie,
So living things can rest sublime,
Now that autumn's nigh.

Brian H Gent

Notes

Divena Collins was born on 29th October, 1940, in Bellshill, Scotland and educated at Bellshill Academy. She came to Watford with her mother at the age of 14 and five years later married Derek. She has two sons, Peter and Roy and six grandchildren.

She enjoys writing poetry and reading other poets' works.

She has a deep respect for the American Indians which inspired her to write the verses of *Geronimo the Brave*.

Geronimo the Brave

The Apache brave stood strong and tall,
He was the greatest of them all,
For love and loyalty to his Indian race,
As he rode to war with painted face.

He fought for Arizona, his tribe's own land,
His name Geronimo he led the band,
There were plenty wounded, blood did flow,
But he rode on with arrow and bow.

It was their home, it was their right,
But still they lost the bloody fight,
A conditional surrender to General George Crook,
As it explains in the history book.

They took him away from his dwelling place,
Geronimo along with his Chiricahua race
To obey the laws of the General's men,
Signed and sealed by a feather quill pen.

They promised he'd return after two years,
To a peaceful reservation with no more fears,
But they broke that promise, the white man lied,
A prisoner for twenty years, before he died.

They say that's how the West was won,
With bow and arrow against fearful gun,
But Geronimo's spirit will stay alive,
For the Apache nation, that now survive.

Divena Noreen Collins

Notes

I am 30 years old, a planning and policy development officer for Leicestershire County Council Social Sciences Department. I was born and lived in West Yorkshire until further education. I now live in Leicester.

I have written poetry since childhood, and started to write more serious, emotional poetry as a teenager. I also write witty poems to share with friends and colleagues. I seldom share the more serious poems - as they are very personal. I have only recently shown them to people.

I tend to write for or about people. Inspiration is usually linked to relationships, especially the more negative and emotional aspects.

I am now very happy in my current relationship, so may be lacking in inspiration for serious poetry for a while!

If You Decide to Let Go

When I reach out to touch you,
You are always too far.
Willing but wary,
To change how things are.
Fearing the feelings,
From a far forgotten place.
Haunted by history,
With emotions to face.
Not ready to feel free yet,
Your heart never cries,
Though it relives feint memory,
When you look in my eyes.
My strength is to steady you
To help break your fall,
My mind is to heal you,
When you answer my call,
Tempting and tormenting me
You are etched on my heart,
A permanent reminder,
Of how I felt from the start.
Your future is hidden,
Your love locked away,
The twist in the tale
Of some mystery play.
The risk is in seeking,
Uncovering the key,
In trusting your judgement
And believing in me.
I long for your closeness,
To share in your pain,
To conquer the hurting,
When you love again.
I long for your company
To touch you once more,
I want to be with you,
When you open that door.
In a life of uncertainty,
There is one thing I know,
My body will bear you
If you decide to let go.

Michelle Bradley

Notes

I'm 38 years old, married to Patricia. We have two children, Shane and Adam, and one due 25th December 1996. I live in Long Eaton, Nottinghamshire and work as a production supervisor. My hobbies are writing and music.

I started writing poetry in my early twenties, but I have been writing since I was eleven years old.

People inspire me to write and a lot of spiritual things do, as well. I try, in my own way, to show the feelings of people and places. I never write for myself; my verses are, I hope, the feelings of a lot of people who can't express themselves.

The giving and receiving of life is so precious, that, when someone asked me to write a poem about it, I jumped at the chance to put pen to paper.

This poem is dedicated to Andrea and Sam, dear friends of ours.

Perfection

Growing inside of me
Is something I can't comprehend
But knowing one day really soon
It will be my child my life my friend
All my dreams have come true
Now my life is about to start
I only wish I could explain myself
I've made a work of art
The meaning of life has arrived
And now my time has come
I'll show warmth I've not shown before
And light up like the morning sun
Perfection is what I've got
Perfection is what I'll breed
I will give to you the gift of life
Please give the love I need
What we have got is life itself
In every shape and form
I'm very scared but very pleased
And can't wait until it's born
My heart jumps out my eyes light up
When I try to understand
What's made from love will soon be ours
And hold perfection in our hand
So please believe me when I say to you
The light will keep us warm
What you gave to me I'll give to you
Perfection in true form

Raymond Spybey

Notes

Jenny Ross, aged fifty, a mother of three grown-up children and the librarian at Upton on Severn library for the last ten years, lives in a Georgian flat, on the eastern slopes of the Malvern Hills, with an inspiring view over the Severn Valley.

Her hobbies include dancing (particularly Scottish country), painting, embroidery and various crafts, growing herbs and lollipop trees. She began writing poetry more seriously in 1996, after attending various poetry gatherings in Malvern.

Valentine's Day

I said I would not write again
But on this day I am allowed
To tell you of my thoughts once more.
You are the man that I adore
And with each day my love grows stronger -
And if sometime, you should remember
In a quiet moment of your busy day,
To spare me one single thought,
It would, in part, assuage the pain of
Unrequited love and of this broken heart.

Jenny Ross

Still Birth

Notes

I am a 31 year old history graduate of Swansea University. Trained as a journalist, I am presently working in arts administration for an independent arts house cinema.
I
have been writing since I was about 17, and my poetry, short stories and reviews have appeared quite widely in this country and abroad, particularly the United States. I am currently working on a novel, and other interests include: sport (rugby, soccer, tennis), music (playing guitar), film and photography.

It's never mentioned.
We do not speak of it.
All evidence of it has been erased.
The cot, the kiddies' clothes, the soft toys, have all been sold.
I've even changed the front bedroom back to how it was
Before we put all that Snoopy wallpaper up.

I've returned the baby's blankets we borrowed.
The pushchair has gone back.
I've buried myself in work.
I've tried to forget.
I've tried not to blame myself,
But I can't help wondering if things would be different
If I'd got you to the hospital quicker than I did.

All talk of babies and children is banned from the house.
They are something we thought of, but can no longer have.
We maintain a dignified silence.
We avoid the subject, steer well clear of it,
But the past still conspires to come between us.

You never gave birth to anything living,
But the miscarriage has still left an emptiness
That cannot be filled,
As if something had lived,
When in fact it didn't.

I try to comfort you with a kiss,
But you just turn your head.
I sense you resent even my touch.
I didn't wish to put you through this,
But it couldn't be helped.
I wish I could make things better, but alas I cannot.

I suggested we adopt, but you wouldn't hear of it.
It wouldn't be the same, you said, if it's not your own flesh and blood.
I see your point, but what other choices do we have?
You have given up and lost all hope.
You say you're now incomplete and it can't be put right.
I accept that.
It's bad enough that we can't have a kid,
But what's worse is they had to cut bits out of you like they did.

Andy Botterill

Notes

I am an 18 year old student from the South West. *Albar* is the first piece of prose I have had published. I began writing poetry early in 1996 - the inspiration for this was the way of taking ordinary, everyday things and turning them into something weird and mystical, strengths which I hope come out in *Albar*.

Albar is the memory of a holiday I took in the Algarve, Portugal. The inspiration came from experiences of the trip and the view from my veranda. *Albar*, the title, is simply the name of a restaurant I visited on my stay.

Albar

From my point above all others
I picture a land I cannot conceive
White pinpricks
Jump from its obscure focus
Giving the area a dream shimmering beauty
Like a late lover's ghoul
Paying last respects.

I see a square of blue
A peaceful, powerful lake
Again the same
Jewelled diamond beauty
Surrounded by a bathing crowd
Of faceless names and strange voices.

In a new sense, I hear
From an uncharted point -
Surreal sounds of a new language
Coupled with a new religion
Blurred, distant,
But with a rhythm that portrays
Wisdom, their white teeth

Gleaming like the huge
Tusk-like styles of their upbringing.
Though on this purity is black,
Only an entrance to further luxury
Its eyes gleaming, black and piercing
On the eternal sleepless night.

From my level I see all this
And many more -
A land I can't understand
But oh so pure it demands respect:
Its culture and traditions so thoroughly right
We moon-child come to visit,
Observe the sleepless night.

John Edwards

The Wonder of Nature

Take time to see the beauty, rest and look around,
Smell the fragrance of the flowers, their colour fills the ground.
Between the tree clad banks, a pond comes into view,
And through the trees and leaves, above the sky so blue.
A place also to wander, to dream, and come alive,
Within this peaceful haven, see the wonder of nature survive.
Dragonflies, their wings shimmering, as they skim the pond,
Darting back and forth then gone, through the trees beyond.
So much to see, to capture, spectacular in sight and sound,
Seasons change, beauty remains and will always be profound.

Irene J Mooney

Notes

I was born in Birmingham in 1944 and have lived in Cirencester, Gloucestershire, for eleven years. Aged 52, I have two married sons and two grandsons. I became a mature student in my late thirties, studying English Language, English Literature and Sociology.

I started writing in my early teens, as I had a need for self-expression, but over the last ten years I have seen my work more seriously, as an emotional and thought-provoking process. Inspiration comes from all aspects of life. I have had several poems published in various anthologies.

My other interests include being a keen member of the Cirencester Operatic Society.

Insomniac

'Tis dark, I waken from my sleep,
To slumber is my wish but through
These lids the half light of day I peek.
The mind races - jumbled thoughts commence,
Where is rest - now is not the time for
Action pray these thoughts will
Get thee hence.

First on my back then on my side, so tired
Yet these wearisome thoughts my brain does rack.
My sojourn on night's balmy sea -
No peaceful slumber through all of
Night is yet to be.
Curse this affliction which caused my
Brain to rock -
'Tis the curse and burden of one
                                        Insomniac . . .

C Clarke

Notes

I am 24 and live in a small town called West Malling, in Kent. I do youth work in the Boy's Brigade and am soon to be married.

I have been writing poems since I was 11 years old and have been a Christian all this time. *The Cat* was inspired by A S J Tessimond and Edward Thomas.

The Cat

The impeccable cat
nearly human as I
she sits by the mat
that once I did buy

Wherever she stroll
secure is her pace
takes the patrol
never showing her face

Feline her gaze
she walks on the rail
boldly and brave
sweeping her tail

She hides in the cracks
safe in her place
she never lacks
the no-need to haste.

Russell J Poynter

Woodstock
(A Cat Much Loved)

Notes

Woodstock was put to sleep in April 1996 (cancer) aged about 16. She had been at death's door when found as a kitten. She gave our family much happiness and joy during her life.

I am married and have one child, Katherine. I'm a schoolteacher (BSc Open University) and live in Loughton, Essex.

I have dabbled with poetry since about 1987 and had one poem published in 1996. Inspiration varies according to circumstances. One poem was prompted by the brutality of Soviet troops in 1991, at the Vilnius television tower in Lithuania.

My interests are reading, travel, folk and classical music and sport. I am a dancer with Chingford Morris Men and an Estonian dance group. My main interest is the folk music and culture of Finland and the Baltic Republics.

Keeping its secret,
That mysterious feline,
She sleeps, and dreams of things
That I can only guess at.

What secret lurks within her mind?
Awakening, she stretches gracefully.
I look deep into her eyes,
Those twin pools of limpid viciousness
Of unfathomable depth.

How can I reach her soul?
Who is whose pet?
What game rules apply
In our daily interactions?
Human questions, untranslatable
Into feline terms.

Could I but see with her eyes,
Feel, hear and smell as she does.
What dimensions could be added
To my experience of life?

Again she stretches,
Her tail gracefully curved
As a pick-up for a (fairground) dodgem car.

A knowing look; a leap;
Two pairs of airborne pincushions
Descend upon my lap,
To wake me from my reverie.

She turns; settles; purrs,
Her mind still closed to mine.

One thing she allows - a gentle stroke
Of her patterned fur, soft to the touch.

C A Last

Notes

This poem is dedicated to my beautiful daughter who died from 'Cot Death' at only nine weeks and four days old.

Another poem dedicated to Louise has been published in an anthology of poems published November, 1996 and a book comprising of letters I have written to Louise, exploring and detailing the real effects and genuine feelings I have experienced since being left as a living victim of 'Cot Death', is due to be published mid 1997.

These three published writings are my tribute to the life and memory of the most precious person to have touched my life.

Louise

A bundle of perfection, so much love inside,
To describe such purity, where does one begin?
A baby full of innocence, of promise and of hope,
A life free from hatred, from destruction and from sin.

A baby born into this world, a miracle itself,
A helpless little person, dependant totally on you.
A promise of the future, a dream you cannot buy,
A love so real, so honest, an experience so new.

You think it is for life, you believe that you have time,
Time to love and to be loved, time to give and take.
Time to learn by trial and error,
Time to correct the mistakes you make.

We take so much for granted, a lesson to be learnt,
For along with each creation given, a life is taken too.
For each truth there is a lie, each touch of joy a stab of pain,
Such simplistic justice, but I never knew.

How can something that's so good induce such bitter heartache?
Someone so beautiful, so perfect, turn the world so dark?
How can such happiness and joy become so quickly sadness?
Someone so tiny leave such a large, indelible mark?

A bundle of perfection, my sweet little Louise,
Love me for all eternity, love me please.

Jayne Rawlings

Notes

I recently became a new mother, which has given me more time to write poetry and is a good source of inspiration. I have had four other poems published in different anthologies. I only started submitting work this year and I am quite pleased with the results and interest shown.

This poem was written on a quiet day in the countryside. I wanted to catch the essence of the wind; I found it both full of passion and lust.

And the Wind Breathed

To me, the wind just breathed today.

Sighing through the trees, kissing the foliage, stirring their passion.

With a strong exhale, inciting a frenzy of unabated vigour, a few seconds of pleasure.

Just out of earshot, the pine trees whispered the finale, the end to a sentence.

Touching, welcoming, to embrace the invisible stranger that rushed from branch to branch, a path of dishevelment.

Disrobing the innocent May petals, teasing them one by one.

Lusting after a rosebud, waiting to snatch it in bloom, the virginity lost.

Unseemly the actions, catching the youth, but waiting the leaves are, to carry their dead.

In a short time now, the funerals will begin, and no longer the wind will just breathe out and in.

J Cross

Mankind's Sickness

I wrote this poem in anger. On June 18th 1981, I realised my misery and hatred were a result of the ego. In fact, all negative emotions - jealousy, greed, shyness, etc - spring from the thoughts 'I', 'me', 'my' and 'mine'. I used mental techniques to become less self-centred; consequently, I found contentment and compassion, confirming my belief that man's true nature is intrinsically pure, but selfish thoughts, like clouds in the sky, prevent the light shining through.

This year, I felt I was returning to my old ways. I wrote *Mankind's Sickness* as a motivation to strive towards selflessness.

If there is no spring in your step,
No sparkle in your personality,
No warmth in your eyes,
No love in your heart,
No compassion in your voice,
No smile on your face,
You're suffering from mankind's sickness.
Your life is meaningless.
Without purpose.
Wake up!
Get up!
Take action!
Look around you.
What can you do?
Who can you help?
What can you give?
Time's running out.
Make your existence worthwhile.
Imagine your epitaph.
What does it read?
A wasted life?
It's your choice.
You can live like a slave
Or you can die for what you believe in.
Think about it!
Have a go.
See what you can do.
But do it quickly.
Death approaches!

Colin Winfield

Notes

I am a mother of three children and have four grandchildren; I was born fifty seven years ago in Edgware, Middlesex. I worked in the War Office on leaving school and then, on marriage, I went to live in North Lincolnshire.

When all my children went to school, I became a senior supervisor at Brumby Comprehensive School. I started to write poetry for family, friends and special occasions, until my family suggested I sent one (about the change of our county in June) away for publication. Since then, I have had seventeen poems published in anthologies and one selected to be put on a cassette of spoken verse.

A Poet

What makes a poet one might say,
A person who loves words with which to play.
Makes a dream come alive on paper,
And leaves a message that one likes to savour.
Gives them sounds to make their minds come alive,
And colours that are around and for them to abide.
Smells that they can imagine or abhor,
Or a vision of a walk beside the seashore.
Wonderful words written down of their thoughts,
For people to read and their imagination they have caught.
Just to give these people a sprinkling of poetic magic,
And to scramble and untangle thoughts into logic.

Valerie Marshall

Sense of Sensing Something Else

Notes

I dislike technology, litter dropped at random, super-market trolleys in rivers, family values abandoned.

I believe in manual labour, and 'Keep Britain Tidy', respect for Mother Nature and God Almighty.

I've never felt so beautifully sad
So high on melancholy
Shared in past years as I fall to the floor
Curled under the table like a cat in a ball.

Hands over my head how far can I go?
Here all alone
Tears on my face streaming down
It's an *under the table world* I've found.

Trembling lips I can't control
Everything I love on hold
So beautifully sad the words I hear
So desperately desperate just as I feared.

I wait for help in my feline pose
How did I get here? Who knows?
I wait for understanding so beautifully alone
So high on melancholy if only you'd known.

Charles Towlson

Notes

Aged 57, married to Sylvia with one son, Daniel; I live in Buckingham. Much of my working life has been spent in creative occupations of one sort or another, but I have only been writing for the past two years.

Among my many interests my hobbies include collecting postcards of Buckingham, collecting fifties memorabilia, home computing, and research of my family history. I founded the Buckingham Camera Club, in 1979, which is still going strong today, with an active membership of about fifty members.

I have written about forty or so pieces, so far, consisting of a mixture of poems, short stories, and one which I call a 'prose-poem', combining poetry proper (rhyming), blank verse and pure prose. I have started three longer novels, plus a number of other poems and short stories in various stages of completion.

Broad Thoughts is a somewhat tongue in cheek observation, borne out of a spontaneous reaction (or over reaction, perhaps) to the insidious and irritating modern evil of political correctness.

Broad Thoughts From Home

Why are *women* so awfully nice
And *wimmin* so awfully not;
It's almost as if they're a different race,
Who range in emotion from icy to hot:
Perhaps they came from a different place
And were never part of the same melting pot
When the world was made.

Men are the same in a different way
And some can be terribly bad,
And even the love which dares not speak its name
And sets them apart in their range and their shame
Is only a part of the name of the game,
Which crosses the spectrum
From saintly to mad.

If you look at a man
When he's young and he's old,
He will look much the same
But more grey;
But a woman in age
Can never assuage
Her young girl's incredible frame.

Young girls in tight dresses,
With long golden tresses
Are a nice kind of species
To be;
But matrons in aprons,
While still being women
Are as different from them as from me.

Tony Webster

Notes

Dedicated to Ms Angela Rafferty of the People's Museum of Memorabilia, Newcastle upon Tyne.

I am working seven days a week in this new museum - it's hectic and exciting and it has inspired me to write poems about it.

My age is - over 60. I live alone at Gateshead. I enjoy reading and writing, walking, dancing and the museum. I am the museum supervisor, guide, and promotional advisor to the boss.

I just like writing as a hobby, but I've had numerous poems published as well as several booklets, and have an Editor's Certificate of Merit from The Society of International Poets, USA.

Museum Games

You are a *gemstone* and a jewel, maybe a star
With an unflawed, long and graceful neck,
Giraffe-like! So certain, so fussy, so sure
As you tower over other small humans. See you from afar,
Who desire to serve you at your beck and call. Oh heck!

From the nature of a happy heart
Joy and happiness permutes, to others impart
A radiance so bright it illuminates
Throughout both day and night
Truly a great and gorgeous sight.

So, to labour with you so bitter-sweet
Gee whiz, oh heck, just another treat
This pearl-stone with the golden heart
Friendly, polite, never offers one fart,
Then there's the café; this

Quaint Victorian scene of treasure
Provides to customers good food and pleasure
From Land's End to John O'Groats,
From afar even sloe-eyed Chinese
All visit to get their oats,

'Cos we ain't shirkers
Good food and drink provided
For us workers,
Some imprisoned in tiny units, alone
Without food or drink,

Parched with thirst, with
Bladders about to burst. Ah!
There's the bucket to
Relieve the pain and tension. It's
Too small, oh f... it; no further mention,

Ah! At last a repast
It's tea, toast and a colette-scone
Iced tea and toast, we give up
After a three hour wait
The appetite has gone,

Oh! Hang on, the scone. Nice bait,
All of this and much more
Duty endured, with devotion
As we work with pleasure
For *our Angie* our lanky treasure,

To close on a power surge, it's best
Red rage RA F - RA F - RAF
From museum to foxholes, power and beauty
Bounce bump and bash that green and concrete verge
Then a prayer of thanks, at the chapel of rest.

Duncan Robson

69

Notes

I am 51 years old with four grown-up children. I live in North London. My hobbies are reading, cooking, handiwork and gardening.

I wrote my first poem three years ago, at a time of crisis and change in my life, as a way to understand and find a perspective behind the path that led me to that point. This poem was published.

The inspiration comes when the heart is open and I want to express an understanding. The inspiration is the understanding. This poem is expressing the simplicity of creation and the realisation of that.

I Dedicate it to my teacher.

Untitled

The flowers within the stony wall
Tall and straight to freedom call
Quiet and still within that place
Sway and call to show their face

I tried to see creation's way
Fit for me to grow and play
On God's own ground is where I stood
Tall and straight I knew I could
To raise my head and meet the day
To sow the seed and grow this way

I stood my ground and saw it all
All perceived around me fall
The day began and so did I
Created sown to freedom fly.

Anne Gray-Thompson

Notes

I was born Macgregor Michael Holmes, on July 8th 1963, in St Albans, Hertfordshire; the son of Michael and Mildred.

I dedicate all my work to my wife Cynthia. We have a four year old son, Boris.

I was first inspired to write poetry by my friend Stephen, in 1986. I think of myself as a psychological poet, whose ideas are a reflection of personal experiences, good and bad. The poems represent a diary of my life and I am grateful for having the ability to express myself in a way that is cathartic for me.

An Empty Space

The pain has healed at last,
And even if the future isn't clear -
I've finally buried the past
By learning to live with the fear.

It's plain to see my life is now an open book
And so is all the shame,
For anyone who cares to take a look -
I paid my dues and took the blame.

From myself I have nothing to hide
And my secrets are out for sure,
But with a friend in who to confide,
I need not ask for more.

Only now am I able to laugh -
For I can barely recall her face.
I used to worship a photograph,
Now all that's left is an empty space.

Greg Holmes

Notes

Born in Barbados, I have lived in England since 1955. In early childhood I wrote short stories and poetry, fuelling my ambition to become a writer. In later years, my nursing career and family commitments took precedence, until two years ago I re-started my poetry, when my quiescent yearning to write came to the fore.

Writing poems gives me a feeling of contentment and fulfilment, as they reveal my innermost thoughts and deepest emotions, which I hope will enrich the lives of others. I also enjoy reading and art.

Dedicated to Sandra and Michael, whose faith and encouragement became the inspiration for my poetry.

Life and Love

Life is a wonderful gift
That goes along with the tide
Intertwining paths and streams are swift
But we must and go along for the ride
We can experience so much joy
By realising *love* is not a toy
Enjoy the best things on offer
Right before our eyes and never suffer

Make *love* and *be loved* our destiny
Which knows no bounds
By being two in paradise
Only to rise
When all feelings are spent beyond the clouds
Where two hearts and bodies unite
On the earth and beyond

The flames of *love* and *life*
Forever burning in the night
Bringing true bliss and happiness
Lost in a caress
Lasting throughout all time
Ultimate *divine love* the sublime.

Cynthia Goddard

Notes

I am a retired civil servant and I live in a village in Gloucestershire. My poem was inspired by visiting my daughter on the Isle of Man. The island has everything portrayed in the poem. It is considered unlucky not to call a greeting when passing over the fairy bridge.

I have had several poems published in various anthologies, and I have always been interested in writing poetry.

My main hobby is flower arranging, but my family (six children and twenty three grandchildren) ensure my life is very full.

The Isle of Man

Anchored in a Gaelic sea
This favoured piece of earth
Only those who dwell thereon
Can really know its worth

Invaded by the Norse-men
In ancient days of yore
A kingdom ruled by Orry
So tells the island lore.

Glens abound in this fair land
Hidden well from view
Crystal streams and pathways
Meandering gently through.

Journey through the uplands
Take the mountain way
A scenic roller coaster
Such a landscape to portray.

A glimpse of wooded valleys
Of waves upon a shore
A mountain top in misty wreath
A gorse encrusted moor.

A bewitching place of beauty
Kissed by fairies so they say
Greetings you must call to them
If you ever come this way.

Eleanor West

Treachery

Join me in the circle.
Sit, apart, on hallowed ground within the ring that is my wedding band.
Cast your eyes upon the gold that flows unbroken round us.
This symbol of my marriage vows becomes a screen to view in sequence
                                        the treachery in my life.
The silent images appear, revolving slowly in dark foreboding.
A family exuberant, alive, moving through the levels of their years,
Experiencing the calms and turbulence of living but knowing love.
The fullness of their being spills over and must surely touch you.
Sense the vibrancy and energy that currents towards us and burns inside
                                        my head.

Do not avert your gaze; your intrusion in our lives demands you bear
                                        with me.
Witness the smiles of indulgent parents - guilt must cause the bile to rise
                                        in rancid streams.
Can you deny the painful pulses that knot and tangle in your gut?
Regard the teasing eyes, a million years removed from painful threat.
Patience! You will soon realise your worth.
Another achievement in an achiever's world.

The screen falls blank, the figures fade, banished to the shades of hurting
                                        shame.
And as I probe your false and condescending smile
I find a well of lonely tears brim full awash upon my soul to dim my
                                        comfort-light
What dreadful legacy is yours? A broken home inherited, translated to my
                                        life?
Did resentment, through the years, at failed pursuit of love
Direct you towards forbidden ground to tear apart the ties of sacred union?

Leave me now. I have used you well.
You have seen a family in disarray and by this confrontation with your sin
Have loosed the dark emotions from my heart and taken them upon your
                                        troubled self.
Step outside the circle which you have desecrated
And spend your barren childless days in ignominy and shame.

E Fitzpatrick

Notes

I am inspired to say that my poetry is dedicated to the Source of All Mankind - the Spirit of God within.

Frustration

I am not a victim - *I am* as God created me
Perfect in every way
And yet, *I* think of who *I am*, frustration is my name
Put in a game *I* willingly play.

Loudly *I* complain of the poor me *I am* - have embodied
A self-fulfilling prophecy,
A victim of unconscious games, *I* don't want to play
Mired in my own decay . . .

The very life *I am* is embodied in those words
Used every day, in every way.
I am this and *I am* that, never thinking what I say
Creating the world *I* see!

So many wrong beliefs from days of old, destroy
The very fabric of my life
Who *am I?* What *am I?*
Frustration is the word *I* give to reap my strife.

We *are* the world, the chaos everywhere we see
Created by unconscious me
Who reacts to life, getting all caught up in the game
Complaining of our tapestry - woven in God's name!

The Holy Self - *I am,* the Word in the beginning
Now is the animal made flesh in materiality
But our very core is Spirit - Infinite Intelligence
Which *I* chose to ignore, and my life a mess.

Carefully now *I* choose my words, they can reap for me
The embodiment of frustration
Before, whenever *I am* saying, feeling or doing as *me*
Is the ignorance and the darkness in the world we see!

Now is the light, the beacon from within
Expelling darkness all around
Self-Knowledge brings understanding it all
No systems are needed when *I am* is *All.*

Joyce Ogilvie

Sour Grapes

I never made it to the top.
I never wanted to.
My life has yielded me a crop
Of sudden drops
And belly flops
And prizes, very few.

So I must be a king or clown
A saint or else a devil.
If there's no up, there must be down
There is no staying level.

Life's ladder climbs up to the stars
So learn this while you're young
If you don't want to skin your arse
Stay on the bottom rung.

Raymond Dunn

Notes

I am more than three score years and ten. I recently attended music lessons and took up the keyboard and now play at the church guild. I have entertained in seniors' clubs for fifteen years doing comedy, reading my own poetry and now, playing keyboard.

I have won the Editor's Choice Award for Outstanding Poetry in 1994, from The National Library of Poetry, America and had seven hymns published in the book, Sing in Praise by Shona Hird, and other poems published in various anthologies.

A Train Journey

Nappies can-can in the breeze
Schoolboy jeans and jersey
Wrestle for supremacy
Shirts white collared
Wave in unshackled ecstasy.

Mary Hudson

Notes

My home is in Glasgow, where I live with my husband, Tony and my sons, Ben (10) and Nicholas (7).

When I'm not day-dreaming about some story or other, to the extent that I drive past my own front door, I teach at a local primary school.

The poem, *Suzanne*, was written in 1996. When my beautiful friend died at the age of 36, she left her family and friends devastated. I have put down on paper some of my most vivid memories of her. She was very special.

I'd like to dedicate this poem to Ashley, Peter and Elliott.

Suzanne

Early morning. Grey skies. Flurry of snow.
8 15. Horn blasts. She's here.
Lovely smile. Sparkling eyes.
Dashing up the path in tartan leggings.
Too early and too cold for conversation.
Kiss my little boy goodbye for the morning.
Put his fat little hand in hers. She pops him in the car.
Off they go. The winter nursery run.

Early morning. Snowdrops bursting from the resting soil.
Clumps everywhere. A solitary daffodil bows in the gentle wind.
8 15. Horn blasts. She's here.
Lovely smile. Hood up. Fur frames her face.
Her elegant hands with painted nails.
It's early, but the gentle start of this day encourages a quick exchange.
Put his fat little hand in hers. She pops him in the car.
Off they go. The spring nursery run.

Early morning. Sunglasses, huge smiles.
Lipstick, earrings - she looks glorious.
Summer, a magnet for all things bright,
And yet, the dark clouds stalk her.
I walk to the gate this time. Too warm not to.
Put his fat little hand in hers. She pops him in the car.
Off they go. The summer nursery run.

Early morning. Orange leaves spiral slowly to the ground.
8 15. Horn blasts. She's here.
We say a hundred silent things to each other.
Bronze eye-shadow - hair with a huge ribbon and enormous bow.
We call her *baby*. She laughs. It's a sad laugh.
So little hair left. The treatment means it's falling out
In handfuls.

Autumn, winter, spring, summer.
It's back. This time when it goes it will take her too.
She battles the fiercest blizzards, the fiery winds, the burning sun, the icy
Blasts of winter.
And then exhausted.
She battles no more.
Early morning. 8 15. No horn. No car. No smile. No red lipstick.
No Suzanne.
My friend.
My friend Suzanne - Goodbye.

Anne Beach

Notes

I was born 10th October 1953 in Zagreb, Croatia. Several of my poems have been published in various anthologies. I think that my poems are funny and joyful. In my poem, I love to capture a moment, a thought, or a detail, and very often something small that people do not even notice.

The titles of my published poems are: *Spring, A Strange Encounter, Could This be the End?* and *What a Grey Day.* The poem, *An Old Bag Lady,* is my fifth to be published.

An Old Bag Lady

I am an old bag lady
An old bag lady am I
I love walking the streets
Och Aye, Och Aye, Och Aye.

Sometimes I find a penny
And sometimes I find three
But even if I don't find any
I am as happy as one can be.

Myrna Smokovic-Campbell

Untitled

Notes

I come from a close, loving family concentrated mostly in the Greater Manchester area. I am currently studying for a business degree. I've been writing for three years and have had several poems published.

Life is one drama after another and sometimes hard to take in. Writing is a useful way of expressing my feelings.

My inspiration comes from many sources, including people I love. The singer/songwriter Bono, and Oliver North - who started life as an honest man but was conspired against by society. I admire his strength and ability to survive his ordeals. It gives me hope.

I feel you in the darkness
Sense you near me at night
So quiet and so still
All I hear are silent thoughts
A living part of my life
Ashamed that I took you for granted
Now you're just a memory
I always wanted you to see the ocean
So many things we never did
I feel bad that I denied you life
Daylight - one big hideous reality
It's then you seem so far away
This town brings out the worst in me
Jealousy, paranoia, claustrophobia
I bend for my soul's companions
All they want to do is break me
It's just too much to understand
Their hateful, wicked mentality
Too often disappointed in love
The devil is on my shoulder
And I succumbed to him at last
My moral nature is falling to pieces
Cynicism is the only thing
That keeps me sane
Someone redeem yourself before me
Can't take this loneliness anymore
And this hate and contempt
That I'm feeling, has to stop
I dreamt of falling from a great height
Maybe it's time for me to jump.

David O'Connor

Notes

I am Chloe Woodford, born 15th July 1952 in Bradford, West Yorkshire. I live in a picturesque village high on the Yorkshire Pennines - in fact not far from Brontë country, Haworth. I am an ex-singer/songwriter and ex-nurse.

My first book of poetry entitled *Simple Poems of Love* is due to be published by The Minerva Press of London in early spring. My poetry is my life story.

The music of Jean Sibelius inspires me and my writings.

The poem *Shame* is based on life.

Shame

And, so to bed,
Cold, cold room
Safe and warm
As in my mother's womb.

Bow my head
To shed a tear
Close my eyes
To hide the fear.

The blanket covers me,
Like a pale muslin shroud,
Anger tears at my heart
Do you have to be so loud?

Go - turn away
Leave me to lay
Pity not my anger
Nor me - my dismay.

Ashes to ashes,
Dust to dust
Fear me - love me
Shameful lust.

For no man
Woman - or disgrace
Shall look evermore
Upon my face.

Chloe Woodford

Notes

I'm Shirley Winskill from Ilkeston, in Derbyshire. I'm married to Gerald and we have one daughter, Suzanne, who is at present living in Cambridge.

I became a poetry 'addict' at the age of seven and composed my first poem when I was a first year child at our local primary school; so I've been writing poetry for most of my life (with long intervals, of course, due to family duties, etc).

I became more prolific with my writing when Suzanne left home and became an undergraduate at the University of Birmingham. I've had around thirty poems published in various anthologies since 1991; many of these have been illustrated by my husband, Gerald.

Moondrift

It was so silent that I could hear
my boots complaining
as they eased themselves from my feet.

It was so quiet that I could hear
my books grumbling on the shelf
elbowing each other for space.

It was so still that I could hear
the snowflakes planting
their soft, sad kisses on the pane.

It was so calm that I felt my thoughts
loosen their threads
and drift to dream with the star children.

Shirley Frances Winskill

A Country Lane

As I was strolling down a country lane,
I suddenly felt at peace with the world,
All cares and worries were cast from my brain.

The birds were singing their sweetest refrain,
The grass and the hedgerows were all dew-pearled,
As I was strolling down a country lane.

Many times I have strolled down this same lane,
And I have seen many beauties unfurled,
All cares and worries were cast from my brain.

I had to keep my many thoughts in rein,
Far away from the troubles of the world,
As I was strolling down a country lane.

I heard overhead a distant jet 'plane,
A reminder of that unwanted world,
All cares and worries were cast from my brain.

My thoughts on all these beauties did remain,
Drunk with the beauty of this lovely world,
As I was strolling down a country lane,
All cares and worries were cast from my brain.

Rosa Butterworth

Teenage Friendship

When Kay and Tess walked home that day,
Slow, funeral-slow were their paces,
It was the funeral of their friendship,
No flowers was written on their faces.

At first, words like horse-hooves
Plodded the September day,
Chummy-talk had ended yesterday;
Still, the blanks called for small-talk.
Awkward pauses - then like crumbs, words
Were thrown out at the singing birds,
But these had no need of crumbs,
Their loves were uncomplicated affairs,
And their songs thrilled the chilling air,
The girls reached Mountjoy Square,
The graveside of their friendship.

'Goodbye, best of luck, Kay,'
'Tess, I wish you someone nicer than John' -

With feelings in control, they walked away
As if they hadn't a care.
A pigeon intoned the funeral service.

Mary Frances Mooney

For a Free Spirit

Notes

Juliet Clare Braithwaite, born in England in 1946, has lived in St Lucia since 1976. She has two teenage sons and has run her own Montessori Kindergarten for ten years. She began writing poetry and stories for children while at St Nicholas' Montessori College in London.

In 1995, she received a Fine Arts Literary Award for a book of poems and an illustrated children's book, entitled *For the Sake of the Children*.

Her sonnet, For a Free Spirit, was inspired by, and is dedicated to, the talented young St Lucian artist who illustrated her book and encouraged her to write.

Where dappled light falls upon the sand
And palm trees dip their heads to taste the sea,
Jagged rocks rise steep on either hand
And sea birds rejoice at being free.
Each time I see these things I think of you
As freedom's aura lights your very presence.
Your art inspired by nature born anew
Shows peace, humility and innocence.
In life we can create or else destroy
The beauty which lies hidden deep within
But you, like spring, bring promise of new joy
Wise beyond your years, brave Paladin!
With friendship comes a truth no man can bend
And we shall have that truth until life's end.

Juliet Brathwaite

Notes

My full name is Paul Anthony Williams. I am 19 years old and live with my mother and two sisters. I am currently unemployed. I used to work for Kwiksave stores when I was a student, studying Business and Finance at Cannock Chase Technical College. I live in Rugeley, Staffordshire.

My hobbies and interests are football and computers.

I have over ninety poems which have never been published. I started writing poetry at college, when I had nothing else to do.

Love and romance inspires me to write poetry. *Dream With Me* is a traditional rhyming poem about one man's love for his girlfriend and how he would dream of being with her for the rest of his life.

The poem, Dream With Me, is dedicated to my girlfriend, Abbie Key.

Dream With Me

I awoke in sunlight splendour,
the dream had come true.
I was with the woman I loved,
which was you.
Dream with me,
until my days are gone.
Dream with me,
make my life last so long.

When we walked on beach's sand.
When we splashed into the sea,
and I held your cold hand.
Dream with me,
until dusk lays its head.
Dream with me,
hold me close in our bed.

This thing is so good and new,
but nothing can compare to it,
than the pure sight of you.
Dream with me,
until this world fades away.
Dream with me,
in heaven, where our bodies lay.

Just dream with me.

Paul Williams

Notes

I am a busy mother of four children, 31 years old and have been married for eight years.

I have always enjoyed poetry and reading, especially as a child, and often used it as a way of expressing my feelings.

This particular poem was written during those 'troublesome teenage years', where sometimes it's hard to make sense of anything!

I hope to continue writing when the children are older, perhaps some poems about children growing up.

Untitled

We can get the answers from the stars
and the questions from the moon.
But the sun she is the only one,
who can tell what will be coming soon.

Whether storm or rain appears,
she will try to hide her shame,
behind the clouds of loneliness
by blotting out the pain
for not being able to find a way
to tell us what will arrive
and whether or not it will last
or if we will survive.

By looking up to the moon
like a father-figure in the sky,
we begin to fantasise what it must be like
to be so far up high.
With only the stars to talk to
as they sparkle by his side,
they give the answers to his questions
and through the night they'll be his guide.

But the sun, unlike the moon,
she must complete her travels alone,
and carry the burden on her shoulders
of not being able to tell what she's known.

Melanie Lane

Changing Times

Things aren't what they used to be,
They're changing ev'ry day;
We can't keep up with each new trend
Before it fades away.
Butter's bad so we eat *marg* -
Then we're told that's wrong -
Eating some eggs will make us ill -
The air's polluted, pollen counts
Are high, and this can kill.
The great computer reigns supreme,
It rules our ev'ry move -
It makes or breaks our characters,
Makes mistakes we cannot prove;
But remember now who works the thing?
It's humans, after all,
Not concentrating on their job perhaps
Or climbing up the wall.
No time to do things properly,
Can't wait to get ahead -
No time to train the youngsters -
They'll watch TV instead.
Not at home to let them in
When they have finished school,
So some go off and turn to crime,
Truant - don't work for any goal.
And while media and press destroy
Our faith in anything,
Slanting the truth to suit their ends
Sensation, drama, scandal rule;
What trouble this can bring.
Is this the world we want to have?
If not, then make a fuss -
Rise from your seat and do your bit
To put things right - it's up to *us.*

J D M Reeve

Royal Navy Socks : WWII

Notes

In 1944, our father was sent out to Bombay. It was the good part of the war for him, as he served on the Philante, a luxury yacht requisitioned from a tea tycoon. Later, after the war, the Government sold it to King Haakon of Norway and it became the royal yacht.

Sometime in 1945, our father was sent to serve with Mountbatten as part of the Burma Campaign. Called 'the forgotten war', it was a terrible time for all those who were now fighting the Japanese in these final months of the war.

Dad was in India
India was always captured in a box
At the bottom of their wardrobe
A box of Calcutta
Images . . . Bombay . . . photographs . . .
Dad in white socks
The same socks that became
Our Christmas stockings
And got lengthened every year
By tugs and pulls
So even more chocolate doubloons
Could fill the toes
And there might be a plethora
Of tangerines.
Not for us the obscenity of pillowcases
Hung up on Christmas Eve
But Dad's India socks
Burma socks
From war zone to home zone.
The wardrobe box
Had held cigars from
Havana
The ones I cut up with scissors
The day he returned . . .
Into tiny bits I cut those
Havanas
Because Mum
Had shut the front room door, shut us out of the return
There was hell to pay afterwards

The only intimacy we ever had
With Dad
Was when we plunged our fingers
Into his India socks
White for Christmas
And searched for doubloons . . .

J Grenfell-Hill

Notes

Pauline Byers was born on the
island of Jamaica in 1954 and
now lives in Derby, with her
husband and young son. A
former college lecturer, she
now works in preventive
health care. *One Man's Chil-
dren* is her first poem and
was written in 1991. Other
inspirational poetry is avail-
able; however, it awaits pub-
lication.

One Man's Children was in-
spired by the notion of equal
opportunities, as suggested by
policies which became very
popular in the 1980's and
early 1990's. It was written as
a result of the injustice she
saw being shown towards an
elderly gentleman in her local
community. The poem is
aimed at reflecting man's
inequality towards each other
and sometimes displayed ig-
norance of our common par-
enthood.

A Christian, her inspiration
for writing this, and other
poetry, comes from acknowl-
edging man's dependence on
God the creator, for direction
and purpose in life. She en-
joys family life, reading,
writing, creative needlework
and leading health based
seminars.

One Man's Children

I am old,
You are young,
My limbs ache with age and I am riddled with disease,
But you are nimble, able and free,
My eyes are dim - glazed with wear,
Your eyes are bright - sparkling, even fair
Your back is straight,
Mine is bent.
Your teeth are your own,
Mine have been lent.
Yet we are all one man's children
I am black. You are white,
My nose is flat. Your nose is straight,
My lips are thick. Your lips are thin,
My hair is short. Your hair is long,
I am a boy. You are a girl,
I am a man. You are a woman,
My eyes are brown. Your eyes are blue,
I am tall. You are short,
I am fat. You are thin
I am ugly. You are beautiful - even handsome,
I own a tent. You own a cottage,
I own a mansion. You own a palace,
My car is old. Your car is new,
Vanity of vanities. All is vanity,
Beauty is in the eye of the beholder,
And God beholds everything,
We are all one man's children
Your speech is clear, articulate and confident,
Mine is simple and plain with a nervous delivery,
Your presentation is grammatically correct,
I present myself how I know best,
My dialect is not always clear,
When you speak everybody hears,
I stammer sometimes,
Your speech flows lucidly all of the time,
I am afraid to stand up and say,
None of this exists in you - in any way,
I have faults you readily see these,
You have faults too,
But, do you see these?
I want to sing,
I am told I can't,
You want to praise God - you can while others can't,
We are all one man's children.

P J Byers

90

Notes

If people meditated upon nature more, perhaps the ills of the world would lessen. My poems, stories and clay sculptures reflect love of animals.

This year, I have had four poems published, having started writing poems in 1993, after the death of a pet.

One aim is to create artwork of sculpture, poem and painting, expressing nature and animals. I have lived in London all my adult life, but childhood was spent in the countryside. I would like to open a sanctuary for animals.

Sixty Six Years Ago

In 1930
A poem was published,
called *Dog o' mine.*
Joe wrote to his dog:
'Remember this - you gave me more
than ever friend gave friend before.'

What greater tribute could there be
to anyone?

Joe's dog knew how to love,
better than the folk he knew.
No one would write that of me.
I should learn from a dog.

Sixty six years hence
and before,
I hope my poem,
published soon
about my dear beloved pet,
will move at least one
to value that most important thing:
the practice of love.

I like to think
that testimony
to my dear pet
could bear a fruit,
after we've gone
sixty years hence.

Joe, I wonder what
you called your dog,
so many times,
before he looked up,
and ran bright-eyed to you?

His name I won't know.
But certain it is
you never forgot
that dog o' yours.

Anna Hall

Notes

I was born in Leek in 1963 and moved to Coventry when I was eleven to live with my father. I left school with no qualifications, married and had three children, all before I was 23 years old. Over the years I have gained various qualifications in further education establishments and I enjoy learning.

Last year, I discovered a hidden talent for art, to my great surprise. I also began to write poetry that seemed to flow naturally. The story of *Anne Frank* has always impressed me and I wrote this poem after reading her diary.

This is my first attempt at publication so it is all new and exciting to me.

Anne Frank

The courage of a very young girl,
has shown me lots of strength,
expressing feelings deep inside
and discussing them at length.

This young girl, righteous and true
sets an example to me and to you.
There is one thing you can't deny
how sad to see her die.

I don't believe there is a one
so young as her above the sun,
and when I see the sun today
I'll think of her in every way.

I can't defend the actions here
of putting her in so much fear
and when I look within my mind
a part of her I find.

I know the thoughts that she possessed
I've heard them in my head,
I've listened to them long and hard
whilst lying in my bed.

And when I think about her age
just fourteen if a day,
most people live a full long life
never seeing things that way.

Wendy Rhead

Notes

I was born in 1971 and live with my parents, who are both retired, in West Drayton. I am currently unemployed

My hobbies include writing, reading, listening to music and watching basketball.

I started writing poetry in 1986, when I was 15. *One,* another of my poems, is being published in an anthology. My inspiration comes from my experiences of the outside world and how I think people feel on the inside - a kind of 'stream of consciousness'.

Pool of Love

Bring us the water
To wash our souls
Bring us the day
To wear our clothes

Only we can find ourselves
In this pool of love -

Pool of love
Splash slowly down
Submerge -
Come on up
Come on in

Take us anywhere
Where destiny is pure
Take us there
Where the tide flows

Only we can know each other
In this pool of love -

Pool of love
Honey on the tongue
Swallow sweetly -
Go on down
Go on out
Into our pool
Of emotional tranquillity.

Matthew Lindley

The English Language

It seems I am old fashioned
To want my verse to rhyme
It seems the days of poets
Have gone with age and time

The beauty of our English verse
A joy to read and see
The beauty of our language
Should be kept by you and me

Our language is our heritage
But as the years go by
It's becoming just for saying
What we think and what we do

In such a very careless way
The words don't mean a thing
They are crude and in most instances
Don't say just what we think

I love the English language
I love the sound of words
I wish I could write sonnets
About the trees and birds

Of the never-ending beauty
Of this our sky and earth
And the ever-changing seasons
On our glorious universe

I would put the words together
To sound as though in song
To be remembered then forever
Not just one's own life long . . .

V M Coote

I am retired and living in North London.

I always wanted to write as a child and won a few prizes for my essays, but I was not encouraged to continue. Some years ago, I won a prize for an essay on pony trekking, but I have never really had time to do any more writing until recently.

My hobbies now are mainly calligraphy, walking and to some extent, photography. Now I am on my own, I find writing poetry relaxing and good fun; it also gives me the chance to air my views in an unusual way. I have had several poems published and feel that I am learning my craft in this way.

My inspiration comes mainly from what I feel about the world around me, and chance overheard conversations.

Freedom

Freedom is the open road with
no more chores to do
where I can wander as I please
feel the sun and kiss the breeze
run through a field of new-mown hay
where poppies in abandon sway

Freedom is my thoughts unchained
by bigotry or hate
When I can muse on things at will
regardless of my fate

Freedom of spirit is the key
to follow where the rainbow leads
over the moon and out of sight
dreaming dreams on a summer's night
That's what freedom means to me.

H Penry

The Unquenched Thirst of Human Superiority

Notes

Creative writing has always been an interest of mine, *The Unquenched Thirst of Human Superiority* being one of a number of poems I wrote whilst at university.

Modern science dictates that life's composition is debatable, never definite.
We can and we do, meddle, tamper, alter so-called imbalances
throughout our world in our tunnelled vision of perfection.
We choose to ignore life for what it is,
that is what separates us from the rest of the animal kingdom.

We deny spontaneity and abstract thought in our search for the concrete.
We pull to pieces life's delicately woven thread
in anticipation of discovering its immaculate make up.
Amateur, we attempt to resurrect, ignorant to the consequences.
Our thirst, (no matter how plentifully quenched) for knowledge
continues to rage.

The consequence?
In his creation of man God has created a time bomb.
His humanistic traits of greed and hypocrisy are dynamite.
The self-destruct button,
        ever looming.

Gayle Leahair

Notes

After a marriage lasting twenty years, and having a partner for twelve years, I now live alone - but am far from lonely. I will soon be 60 years old, when my intention is to semi-retire. I am a registered care manager and live in a lovely riverside house in the Forest-of-Dean.

My sons, their partners and my lovely grandchildren enhance my life.

My love of writing poetry started when I was 13 years old and has continued over the years. Two of my poems have been published.

Family and friends are special to me and over the years have been my source of inspiration. I live my life trying to be non-judgmental, with a positive leaning towards people less fortunate than myself.

Grandad's Old Brown Stick

It hangs there in the corner
Looking quite forlorn
It used to be a treasure
Now it's old and worn

It's travelled every unknown place
Through hail - rain and snow
No matter where dear Grandad went
The old brown stick would go

In the golden summer time
They'd walk the lanes together
Over fields - climbing hills
Caring nothing for the weather

Now that Grandad's passed away
Those walks will not be had
I feel certain at times when I go by
That the old brown stick looks sad.

Shirley Davis

The Second Time Around

Notes

I am a retired widower, residing in Hornchurch. I often record poems I have composed on tape, for the Talking Newspaper for the Blind.

I myself have been registered partially sighted, but this has given me a wider outlook on life. Although I have been writing poetry for many years, I now see things in a different light; I see people differently.

A very charming lady gave me the thoughts and influenced me in the writing of this poem. People who know of love will understand.

When one has loved and one has lost, the Lord has taken them to rest
Knowing not which way to turn, nor what to do for the best
You feel your life is empty, no reason left to live
You feel that you have given your all, and there's nothing more to give

You walk, you work, you look around, the void is always there
There's no reason to be alone, not when there's love to share
For that love it could be strong, the second time around
So join hands and take a chance, on the new love you have found

Only those in love who saw you, would know just how you feel
They would not laugh or make fun, of the kisses that you steal
Only time is what you need, to make changes in your life
Never challenge the sands of time, get together as man and wife

These words are often spoken, when love again is found
So take heart make a new start, *for the second time around.*

Eddie Green

Third World

Notes

I was deeply moved to write this poem after having seen pictures, on the television, of the plight of the people in Africa, but, as a Christian, I believe there is hope as I read my Bible. Revelation, Chapter 21, verses 1 to 8: There will come a time as it is written when the whole world will be a better place.

So much poverty, so much sorrow
Seemingly no hope for tomorrow
Pathetic little faces staring around
Sitting crouched down on the ground
Children with no hope of anything better
Famine, flies, dirt the disease setter
So it goes on, one wonders
What on earth can be done
Such a huge problem, that's gone on
Through many generations
Although people from different nations
Do what they can and unite
Still the terrible plight
Of these people is hard to put right
There is a hope in sight
When Jesus comes again to reign
The world will be a better place
For each and every race.

Dorothy Price

Notes

I wrote the in-store monthly magazine for staff information during my working years and retired ten years ago, aged 60. I found my writing talent useful for the women's group I belonged to, and wrote press reports and many limericks, to familiar tunes, and poetry for the concert party.

I was widowed fifteen years ago and married an artist in 1989, which found me writing poems to complement his pictures.

I have had two separate stories printed in two books on local history. Recently, I learned how to use a computer and am now the proud owner of a printer.

At the age of 70, I am pleased to get inspiration to write poetry and children's stories, etc.

I am looking forward to seeing one of my poems in print.

Untitled

As I looked in the mirror today
Seeing my furrowed brow
I wished that I was twenty one
And as wise as I am now

Going to work in a retail store
I wonder how I'd be rated
Decided I don't think I could
Those tills look complicated

To be in an office things have changed
I am sure I would need a tutor
I know now that it is no good
I'd have to use a computer

Even the lads today have changed
A love bite on the ear was endearing
But it's no good today you couldn't do it
You'd get a mouthful of earring

There's too many changes and complications
I'm not as wise as I thought
Where's my book and reading glasses
The bag of sweets I bought.

Jessie Berry

The Drownings

Notes

I have been married for thirty years to Robert Dye. I'm a hospital receptionist and have lived most of my life in central London, where my husband was a police officer.

I have always been interested in writing and have had many items published in various magazines and papers, including the Sunday Times. I love writing poetry, as I can express my feelings more freely than in speech or prose.

The Drownings was written following the drowning of two friends, a mile from the beach at Bognor Regis.

I stood upon the promenade and watched the sea.
The waves rolled darkly, huge and menacing,
Then broke with fury onto the shifting beach,
Throwing cold spume high into the sky
Before rushing back again, downwards, out of reach
To gather fresh momentum, and with each thrust
Pound the rolling stones into sand and dust.
An angry sea, harsh and unyielding,
Ready to swallow up anything in its path,
The kind of sea that has since time remembered
Shown little mercy to those who risked its wrath.
I saw a wave rise up, and in its darkness
I thought I saw the faces of friends that drowned,
Dead faces, reflected in the very water
That robbed them of their life and claimed them as its prey . . .
The wave dashed the ghostly images at my feet,
And I believed the wetness on my face was just the spray.

I came again and stood and watched the sea.
This time no thunderous roar or frightening fury,
Just tiny waves lapping to and fro in play.
The sands were warm and wide and friendly,
Stretching as far as I could see along the bay.
On the beach the sun had bleached and dried
Flotsam abandoned by the fickle tide.
A peaceful sea, innocently blue and glistening,
Softly ebbing with a rippling sigh,
Seagulls floated lazily in the shallows
Pecking idly at the weed that drifted by.
But I looked deep into the calmness of the water
And once more I thought those faces lingered there,
Pale faces, gone forever in that now tranquil water
That when tempestuous had dragged them down to die . . .
My dog played happily at the water's edge,
And no one noticed when I began to cry.

Anita E Dye

101

Notes

I am a student at St Edmund's College, Ware, in my final A level year. I have aspirations to be a pilot in the Royal Air Force.

I started writing poetry in September 1995. I write when I am depressed, because it helps me to express my emotions without having to go to other people with my problems. My poems are simply about the everyday emotions of a teenage student.

For the Best is about gentle, yet transparent rejection from a girl who has already let things go into the relationship phase, without really wanting to. She has led the person into thinking things are fine and then turns it all around. She gives lame excuses such as 'It's not you, it's me'. These just aggravate the person even more. He can't understand why this is happening to him and is not satisfied with friendship, or her decision that it is 'for the best', when he quite obviously thinks it isn't.

For the Best

'It's for the best' she said
but I'm upset, I feel misled.
'Women!' my mates say,
that doesn't help at the end of the day.
One of their kind has tricked me again,
my mind is clouded over, one thing in my brain.
Why? It was going so well,
I wonder as I return to emotional hell.

'It's not you, it's me' she said,
that doesn't help it just wrecks my head.
I'd rather it was me then I could change,
to cut off emotional ties for no reason, to me, seems strange.
'Why?' It's useless to question her,
she's made up her mind as to what she'd prefer.

'We can still be friends' she said,
Yeah right, like that's better instead.
There's nothing I can do, so why get upset and worry my little head?
'After all it's for the best' she said.

Thomas Ball

Matilda

Notes

I am 76 years of age, married
with one son and a grandson.
I live in Brighton and am a
homemaker and writer. My
autobiography, The Days
Grow Short, was published in
May 1996.

I have been published in
many poetry anthologies and
was awarded an Editor's
Certificate of Merit from The
International Society of Poets,
in October 1996.

I started writing poetry last
year. My inspiration is per-
sonal joy and sorrow, and the
beauty of nature.

Matilda was a real Zulu lady,
whom I employed and grew
fond of while living in South
Africa, so I suppose my poem
is dedicated to her memory.

I lived in South Africa for a while,
And one day thought I may employ
Someone to help my leisure time to enjoy.
There was a Zulu lady standing at my door,
Requesting work, part-time or more.
'I'm Matilda,' she said.
Obviously well read, I thought,
I really ought to secure this one,
From then on, we had tremendous fun.
Using hand-signs to comprehend our speech.
Then there was a ghastly drought,
No water in her compound was about
For families to drink or use.
I got two vacuum flasks out and filled with
Ice-cubes, I drove her back to her habitat.
'Oh Missus,' she says, 'For this you
Can be confined to your home for ninety days!'
'Don't risk your freedom, rain must surely come.'
Said I, 'Why won't someone care?'
She said, 'Jesus does, that is why I say a prayer.'
She had no bitterness for Government of old,
Her skin like velvet, black.
Her heart was made of gold.
There should be regret for Matilda's life
That was not free.
Cruel injustice. Apartheid is the word to use for you and me.
And we will all understand that change must stay
In that fair land, South Africa.
Where Zulus, and other tribes, and yes, the whites,
In peace will survive, and all be glad to be alive.

F G Tester-Ellis

Notes

I would like to dedicate this poem to my Father, who couldn't accept this life, and to my Mother who has.

I am 21 and started writing poetry when I was 15. I find it a great release and comfort.

I am inspired by everything around me, but mainly by people and their unique characteristics.

Having graduated this summer with a degree in English and History of Art, I now have a job in interior design. However, I still intend to travel and write about the various cultural differences that I find. Having studied non-western art and culture this would be particularly interesting for me.

Silence Pounds

Silence pounds in my head
Outwardly pushing my memories of you
And now only my heart is burning and full
Of sadness at the desperation you knew.

So your hand crept shakingly closer
To the switch between your life and death
Your finger, the thief, took you from us -
For you the escape a chance to rest.

Did the birds that flew to the trees
With fright from the sound of that gun,
Did they hear your wistful breath's falter
As your tears dried in the heat of the sun?

The echo must have lingered for hours
As it mingled with the sound of her scream
And you lay silent and peaceful forever
The solution to your lifetime's bad dream.

But daddy, my daddy, you've left us
Sometimes anger's the emotion most strong
It doesn't seem right that you suddenly went
And I ask, 'What did we do wrong?'

Was your mind so beating with anger?
What drove you away, so afraid?
This world wasn't perfect in your eyes
Now it's deeper plunged into grey shade.

The silence and love will still linger
In our hearts that never seems to dim
But my memories, I'm sorry they're fading
As idealistic images set in.

Catherine Spring

The Last Drop

Notes

This poem is written about a young man searching for lost friends in an effort to find an anchor of happiness. A fictitious piece of absurdity of someone 'demobbed' in 1946, trying to pick up where he left off years before, but realising it's impossibility.

It is an attempt to introduce a note of humour into what was supposed to be a celebration - and indeed it was - but which could easily transform itself into an absorbing sadness.

Knowing how to laugh was in his favour. The trick was keeping it spontaneous so that it became a meaningful therapy. And it did.

Meandering through the village of Waddling-by-the-Water
Which nestles in the vale of Dunging-Ditch,
I thought of Middle-Humpton and the vicar's only daughter
And the curate known as Billy Littletich.
She met him on the choir trip to Higher Fetlock-Bantham
As he cycled up from Crumbling-on-the-Green.
Through Lower Shelving-Bottom, he pedalled like a phantom,
But at Muck Hill had to walk for lack of steam.
I wandered on and headed up to Cocklebury Way
Along the towpath passing Scratchit's Lock,
Then down by Piddler's dairy farm, not far from Treacle Bay,
To imbibe the amber brew, while taking stock.
On I went up Hangman's Hill to Watling-Stupple village
Down Goosey Lane which feeds on to the green;
To Nellie Racker's corner, the scene of ancient pillage
Which leads to meadows down by Crumpet Dene.
By turning left at Gallows Cross, I headed back to town
Through blacksmith Benny's forge near Flatiron Cottage,
Then a fast and foaming pint at the favoured Rose and Crown
And a bowl of landlord Barney's steaming potage.
At Wilton-under-Lay I gave consideration
To a pint of Old Peculiar in The Cloggers,
Which gave a quiet confidence and sheer determination
As I headed for The Woolpack with the joggers.
Down to Friar's Tavern for a half of better bitter
Then, across the road to Fiddler's Cyder Bar,
Whilst the Laughing Monk and Nun, next door to Joe's bedsitter
Sold a potent lager known as Happy Jar.
It soon became apparent as I left the Muffled Trumpet
I had now become an alien to sobriety;
So a pint of Black and Tan despite attention from a strumpet
Gave the well oiled wheels a sense of real propriety.
I fell into the Hare and Hounds, the Horse and Jockey too,
But was thrown out of the Grapes and Golden Fleece!
So I tried the Market House and then the Waterloo
And got a helping hand from local police!
All in all, it seemed to me, I'd had a most successful day
As I sank a pot of Brewers' Old and Jolly.
A swift half in the Rovers with a ploughman's on a tray
Then home - before things got too melancholy.

Ray Butt

Notes

Although born in South Africa I now live in Perth, Scotland. I have been writing poetry ever since I was a wee girl. My first poem to be published was in the book, *Midlands Today,* in 1992. My second, *First Love*, was published in *Growing Pains,* in 1993.

I enjoy writing poetry for my own pleasure, as a hobby, along with painting and studying. This particular poem was written light-heartedly, about vain people in society (myself probably included in that!).

Untitled

Suddenly, as I walked into the room,
I noticed her -
the long auburn hair, those deep cerulean blue
eyes, her smile captured my soul, thrusting
reality aside with an enchanting angelic
beauty rarely seen. She had an elegance
enclothed in grace.
Oh the epitome of finesse so divine!

And as I stared, dazed by her aura,
someone *abrupted* such a sweet moment, to
remind me of the fact -
I was gazing in a mirror, at that!

Amanda Reason

Notes

I have been interested in poetry, literature and art since attending Enfield County School. I am married to Chris, a chartered engineer, and we have three grown-up children: Amanda, Nick and Paul, and also three grandchildren, Robert, Freddie and Molly.

I am 54 and live in Frimley, Surrey; I started writing poetry for family and friends about twelve years ago. Many of the recipients suggested submitting poems for publication; advice I never heeded until now! I wrote this particular poem for my sister, Annette - a fellow poet - in National Poetry Week, last year. Other interests include travel and photography.

The Spirit of Autumn

I was sitting in my garden, on this golden afternoon -
Observing the summer flowers, which now have lost their bloom.
The sunlight cast long shadows - it is that time of year -
I cherish these precious, autumnal days, too few of them, I fear.
The acorns dropping softly, upon the mossy ground -
As the squirrel gathers his winter's store, then buries it, safe and sound.
The azure sky, above my head, contrasts its vivid blue,
With russet tones of leafy trees, of every shade and hue.
And as I dream and drift away, comes soft upon the air,
The heavenly chorus of birdsong, no composer, wrote so fair.
Oh! That I could freeze in time and place, this feeling of warmth and peace
And then the strivings within my breast, would quieten, be still - cease.
So I wish for you, my love, the magic of such a day -
And hope eternal be released and sent along your way -
Like the brilliant sunflower, Van Gogh immortalised with his art -
Capture the spirit of autumn, and place it firmly within your heart.
For each and every season, brings its own sweet prize -
Just open up your senses and use your keenest eyes.
Take comfort from the rhythm of the marching months -
Don't miss a beat, or falter, no; not even once.
And then I'm sure you'll survive, winter's icy blast -
And *springtime*, will be here once more, with happiness to last.

S J Brooks

Notes

Anthony Higgins (Tony) was born 31st March 1949, in Brondesbury, London. He is a retired civil servant and is now a carer for the elderly.

He has had two poems published, to date, and forthcoming poems are to appear in Poetry Now and Poetry in Print.

Inspiration often comes from the way people act and behave in this mad world we live in. As a wise person once said, 'Who watches the watcher while the watcher is watching?'

Suburban Tussle

Back to the days of trouble and strife
Travelling by train to work with the wife
Trying to board the carriage with arms in the way
Pushing and shoving to get on this day
Doors close behind squashed in like a net
Now one knows what it's like wearing a corset
Unable to breathe or move a muscle
No good anyone having a tussle
Doors open at next stop everyone falls out
Like a wrestling match into the next bout
Down to the tube via escalators or stairs
Originally started off on the way in pairs
Lost in the furore getting to one's station
Or though at times lost that inclination
Why does one do it day after day
There must surely be a better way
Work nearer home if only one could
Strike if you like it really does no good
Arrived at work completely worn out
Another day tomorrow, back on the roundabout.

A T Higgins

Fishing Holiday

Och, slowly slants the rosy dawn
On a braw and bricht Heilan' morn,
Where at break o' each new-born day
A stalwart Sassenach makes his way,
And sits him down on his little stool
Beside Lochlarnie's deepest pool,
And hopes that e'er the day has died
He'll gang back hame wi' joy and pride,
And that in his brand new creel will rest
The biggest, bonniest o' the best,
And that he'll nae be at fault
Tae sup a glass o' single malt,
While that frying frizzling sound he hears
Is joyful music tae his ears;
For well he kens that bonnie silver fish
Wad make the tastiest supper dish.
But eh puir lad! All day he whups that pool in vain -
Those cunning fish his new-fangled flies disdain,
Sae he'll gang back hame wi' weary tread,
And kens he will, instead,
Sit down wi' many a heart felt sigh,
And dine once more on cottage pie.
Och, braw laddie! Do ye nae ken
'Tis only a Scotsman, the bravest of men,
Can leave his bed at break o' day
And with lively steps, wend his way
O'er dew-wet or frozen grass
Wi' a heart that's bound wi' three fold brass,
Tae where in Lochlarnie's pool sae deep
Those lazy fishes lie asleep?
Only a canny Scot has nae long to wait
Before one wakes and takes his bait.
He kens that he can make them rise
Wi'out using artfu' flies.
Sae bonnie laddie! 'Tis nae crime
Tae gang back south, and fish from the pier
At Brighton or some place near.

Margaret Thomas

Notes

I have been writing poetry for
approximately twenty years. I
am mostly inspired by nature,
especially its colours and
sounds. I am also inspired by
the English language - words
can be so evocative.

Winter

And now the winter wind doth blow
once more we see the virgin snow
filling dyke and dell to brim
resting its beauty so neat and trim.

Children playing - happy with mirth
enjoying pleasures for all they're worth
a snowball here a toboggan there
a slide or snowman for all to share.

The trees that once were dressed in green
now stand white - elegant - tall and serene
again the snow falls softly down
covering the hedgerow as if with a crown.

H Cullum

Man and Moon

Notes

I'm a retired housewife; I live in Barry, South Wales, and I love it.

Convalescing after major surgery, I looked up my early poetry, sent some of it off and had it all published. I have now been short-listed in a national poetry competition.

All aspects of life fascinate me, and the wonder of existence.

I study 'English' literature, but my heart throbs for Wales and its Welshness.

Now sadly this century
Ends, so far from early man;
And with myriad regrets,
Time unwinds his sacred span.
Oh! Folly is man's wanting,
Of this truth you must agree,
For with one foot, one step, he
Killed a living mystery.
Then swiftly the seraphim
Astronauts ascended. The
Man craving rockets to the
Firmament high above, and
Then with lust descended;
Defiling the moon we love.
Taking away our secret
Trust, by forever spoiling
Our virgin moon's dust; for he
Was always much a part of
Man's pathetic lonely heart.

Sonia Ruckley

Notes

I am 13 years of age and attend Leek High School. I live on a dairy farm in Rudyard, Staffordshire, with my parents. I have an older brother and a younger sister.

I enjoy sport and I swim and play rugby for my local town. I started writing poetry about five years ago, encouraged by my speech and drama teacher.

Hallowe'en

Children running down the street,
Shouting out loudly *trick or treat*.
The elderly are huddled in their homes,
Listening to the awful groans.
Witches fly across the sky,
Whilst families eat pumpkin pie.
Lanterns shine their amber grin,
And children eat pomegranate seeds with a pin.
Ghosts howl and scream through the night,
Keeping people indoors until daylight.
Spiders and bats are everywhere,
Giving everyone a huge scare.
Apple ducking is the bit I like best,
But I know Mum thinks I'm a pest!
Water, water everywhere,
This is great fun and I don't care!
Roast chestnuts are so nice,
I've only had them once or twice.
'Tis a shame that Hallowe'en only comes once a year,
But it's great excitement when it's here!

Alexander Rider (13)

Notes

I am single, currently living on my own after enjoying (or not enjoying) but no longer regretting, a five year relationship I started in the late eighties. My bungled attempt at settling down!

I am 32, a tradesman and I have lived and worked in Leeds all my life.

My inspiration for *Leaves* reflects my coming to terms with myself over 'that five years', and also the influence of walking in Goldenacre Park, Adel, Leeds, often with friends I took there to see the lake, the swans and the flora; a credit to Leeds City Council parks and leisure services.

If I am not enjoying the pleasure of the park, then maybe I am at the pub or at the theatre, or perhaps on one of my epic bicycle rides.

I dedicate Leaves to Dawn Parker.

Leaves

The wind in the trees sends the leaves falling, swirling, swirling
and something deep inside tells me the tide is turning
no more can I hide from what I am so quickly learning.

The day enters the night and my insight is awoken
no longer need I fight or consider I am broken
now as each day begins I see little of before
I contemplate new beginnings and more.

So the sun sets again and I reflect on one more day
seems yesterday was the same
but who am I to say
what tomorrow will bring, because I'm going all the way.

The wind has gone silent now and yet it tells me somehow
it will always be around,
around the next corner something may be found
and if I give up looking I will become
the leaves, fallen to the ground
but my affinity lies much more with the trees.

The trees that stand the storms
grip the earth harder more and more
and the seas may lash every port and shore
so brief is our existence.
Life's too short to count the score.

I walk in the park, around one golden acre
and the pleasure of it all tells me much of its maker
poor is he who cannot appreciate this beauty and all of nature
as it costs me nothing but the effort to look and see.

I am not so blind to want to be the tree
and maybe soon I will blossom again
gone with the wind my woes and pain
into the sunshine out of the rain
the leaves decompose
yet the tree, like me, remains . . .

Steve Thaxter

Like Wine

Notes

I am Susan Fenn, 40 years old, born in South Wales and moved to London when I was 11 years old. I'm married with three children, aged 19, 14 and 12. I work at a local school and live in Eltham, South East London.

I enjoy writing, drawing and watching sad films with my daughter.

My other published poems have been written for children. My family are always patient and make me laugh which, nowadays, is so important.

I dedicate my poem to them, for supporting me in whatever I do.

Eruption causes the face
to flush with,
loss of control.
I enjoy the control
you are mine.
Without you, I would be,
like an empty glass of wine.
Consumed, the pleasure
empty,
waiting,
waiting a while for my glass
to be filled.
Emotion and pleasure overflow,
like the pause and hesitation
of doubt.
Shall I drink and even drown in the pleasure
awaiting me,
or,
shall I sip,
the glass of wine.

Susan G Fenn

Notes

I live in Hull, Yorkshire.

Half Cat was published in 1989 and was dedicated to my granddaughter, who asserted that she shared my cat, Bonnie. I have written several other poems on various themes, some being broadcast on Radio Humberside, and five have been accepted for various anthologies this year.

Also this year, I have received a certificate and shared second prize in a competition. I wrote an article on earlier years as PA to the manager of the then Repertory Theatre, telling of future stars: James Mason, Maurice Denham, Noel Howlett, etc.

My main hobbies are cat portraits and landscapes. I first attempted to write seven years ago, when becoming disabled with arthritis.

Inspiration comes from memories of holidays abroad, nature and animals. *Lighthouse*, about two lighthouses in Bermuda, recalled how important these features were for sailors, long ago.

Lighthouse

Towering high, snout to the sky,
A lonely giant he,
Feet encased in sand and rocks,
Spiral stair, his knee,
Gaze out-distance the sharpest eye,
Beam encompass the sea.

From far away, men monitor his mood,
Should they forward or stay,
Slight mistake and they cower in fear,
Wrath to keep at bay,
On his help their existence depends,
Should he waver, then dire dismay.

Encircling base, the lashing waves,
Rush then leave him be,
Whirling mass of stones and shells,
Twist, twirl, then back to sea,
Wise, as one who has ruled so long,
Advice ignored, extracted fee.

Sailor, fisherman, on him depend.
As guardian of the sea,
A mighty master of wind and wave,
Their guide and mentor he,
Reflecting hope or swift recall,
Shafting light, safe landfall.

Grace Wade

Last Visit

Notes

D Elizabeth Smith is retired
and has had a few poems
published in anthologies.

Last Visit evolved after many
happy walks in the Peak Dis-
trict with her dog and family.

The old man,
sat beside the stream
that rippled down
the craggy glen,
sun warm on his back,
grass soft under feet.
His eyes traced undulating green,
scattered rocks and sheep,
how many times,
how many years,
he'd climbed the path
to sit alone
high on the hill,
to rest and think and dream,
his own small place,
undisturbed by human race,
by modern ways.
He'd fought a war
his only thought,
to keep forever free,
this sweet retreat
that tirelessly
refreshed his soul.
His frail frame, sat unmoving,
gazing long, a contented spirit
making its last visit.

D Elizabeth Smith

Notes

I was born in Leicester in
1959 and have lived here all
my life. I am a factory worker
and enjoy writing poetry in
my spare time.

Shadows of the Night

Cassie sat down heavily on a rickety
Old wooden chair that creaked and groaned
Under her weight and grimly stared at
Her reflection in the dressing-table mirror.
She ran a hand through her short black
Hair and rubbed her sore red eyes.

A cold wind whistled through rotten
Window frames making them rattle and
Cassie shivered as she snorted fine,
White powder. Dead eyes twinkled with
Life again and for a short while she'd
Feel no pain.

Cassie used to think she'd have a nice
Life, maybe one day be somebody's wife.
She thought she would be happy.
But now she knows there will be no
Roses round the front door, no children
Shelling peas on the lawn, no fun for
Her, no morning in the sun.

Anaesthetised, she steps out onto white
Frosty slabs glistening in the moonlight
And disappears into the murmuring shadows
Of the night.

David Sarson

Forty

Notes

I am 59 years old, married for 37 years and have two sons who are both also married. I have three granddaughters (is the name of Jones headed for extinction!). I grew carnations for a living for thirty years, which was abruptly ended by my bank's intervention. This was followed by ten years of planning revenge on the bank and landscape gardening.

I have written since schooldays, when I was almost expelled for exposing the entire idiosyncrasies of the teaching staff in a school play.

I have had several articles published, and one poem in an American anthology.

Although I write mainly in a humorous vein, I believe that poetry is the most powerful medium to express all human emotions.

It is the watershed of another of life's phases.
The slow dawning that youth will not last forever.
A time when the joints begin to stiffen, and a muscular
stroll along a crowded beach becomes a conscious contrived thing.
A time when the lungs put limitation on physical endeavour,
time the leveller.
The body, which shape appeared a constant thing, sagging,
rings its warning bell.
Now the decisions must be made, to fight on and gain some
years of grace, with diet, exercise, and walks at pace.
Or perhaps to just give in and thicken comfortably to old age.
How then to decide your chosen path. Look around you
on that beach and see if others' ways can give direction.
What effort needed for the portly man to rise from the
water up that stony slope, but laughingly his rounded
wife gives him a tug, and seated in a groaning canvas chair,
resumes his eating to old age.
Now from the water comes a better shape, a man well over fifty,
attracting female glances, but could he respond to their
advances? Yes, I believe he could, a man who has done the
things he should, returns to the towel spread on his stony
bed, and dons his yachting cap upon his head.
I look now at my slightly younger wife, still beautiful,
a flower full-blown in life.
Which path will she take, I wish I knew, if she got fat
then I could get fat too.

T W Jones

Notes

My home was in Victoria, Vancouver Island, British Columbia, Canada, until I came to England with my parents and sister for a summer holiday, after finishing our schooling.

Since then, there have been travels and the making of homes and gardens in various countries, though England has remained my adopted base. I now live in Sussex and feel that perhaps I have at last retired!

Poetry writing is new to me. It is only this year, after an illness, that I suddenly found myself, almost compulsively, 'writing' poems in my mind, and very soon realised the need to write them down as they came to me. This I have been doing since February 1996, and *Dreams* is one of them.

Dreams

Where else to go where life may cease
And yet where life begins?
It's when you close your eyes in sleep,
And conscious life is stilled to keep -
Yet cannot halt your sleep's release
From worlds it does not know:
For here, like space, are mysteries - sometimes filled with woe -
That no one else across the globe,
Of wide-spread lands and seas can probe,
Because yours is now a scene unknown -
A world of colours where you've flown
Without propulsion - yet here you stand with strangers, all alone!
And, too, there're friends from near and far -
(They're driving 'round in your new car!)
They gather, laughing, having fun!
While sometimes - darkly - mischief's done . . . !

Behind your sleeping eyes the visions seem to drift - they form some
                                                        fearsome things,
Menacing your night on misshaped spreading wings
Which fall, broken, from the sky -
Their Cyclops pilots have one eye! And yet none,
Not even you - show surprise at what is done!
The scene is changed: here comes the sun with pets from long ago!
Cats who play, while swans glide by where rivers gently flow.
Where country lanes are twisting roads
That make a path for travelling toads! The picture now fades on:
For just as eyelids slowly blink and night is nearly gone,
There looms a face you think you know - but why is it a crow?
Quietly now, you turn again - you sigh to see the moonlight wane.
Do not regret your world of dreams - they come to soothe life's irksome
                                                        seams:
Where else to hide from reprimand? Where to live without command?
Where to love and to remember?
So be courageous - be sincere - not for you a lost pretender!

D R Payn Le Sueur

Orange

Orange so juicy so bright, so warm
Like the aftermath of a thunderstorm.
Brilliant enchanting a complete all in one,
When red and yellow together they come.

He will savour the moment at climax of summer
When he's crushing the darkness making it gone.
Changing me from a subtle pinkness of pale
Penetrating deeply like a twelve inch nail.

Breaking intaking drowning the body
Of something so innocent tender and cold.
Testing molesting the skin of a pale back,
To changing of flowing of brown in gold.

Rehearsing conversing with an almost friend,
Holding controlling to meet an almost end.
Testing molesting holding all back,
Perversing and breaking in on her soon.

And stealing love in orange.

Eddy Ferguson

Fear

Notes

I was born in Scunthorpe in 1965 and work as an office manager.

The poem's about not letting your decisions be dictated by the fear of the possible consequences. If you want something, you have to do all you can to achieve your goal, and not be afraid of what might go wrong. Because most people don't like taking risks, they choose the safe, sensible option and therefore, may never find out what could have been possible.

The inspiration for this was the decision to move back to England after having lived in Holland for twenty years.

I don't want to be guided by fear
But it's always there
It's always near
It comes to visit in bed at night
And it won't be vanquished by the morning light
Fear's an enemy
Fear's a foe
Drink can fight it
But can't make it go
Love can help
But love always fades
And when love's gone . . .
Fear invades.

Guy William Thomas

Notes

Born in France 1912, I studied at the Conservatoire de Paris. I became broadcaster for Radio Algiers during the Second World War, directing and writing children's programmes in both French and Arabic. As a member of SACEM (Societe de Auteurs et Compositeurs de Musique), I conducted in concert. As a British citizen living in England since the war I joined the PRS (Performing Rights Society). I have composed and orchestrated music for films and ballets. Having been a music teacher at Roedean School, Brighton, I am now retired.

This is my first attempt at writing poetry in English and has been inspired by my great love for music and language.

Ballad for a Departing Musician's Soul

There was a beautiful sky, that night; surprisingly . . .
After the rain subsided; shyly . . .
The musician looked at the rainbow, up there; longingly . . .
Extending eager hands, he caught hold of it; delicately . . .
The rainbow would make his lute; hopefully . . .
A spangle of dew could be his string; possibly . . .
He started strumming his magic instrument; lovingly . . .
Extracting extraordinary sounds that no ear perceived; unfortunately . . .
Expressing the struggles on the battleground of his soul; painfully . . .
Two lost harmonics escaped his trembling fingers; wastefully . . .
Disappearing like flying stars; completely . . .
Tears rained from his bewildered eyes; constantly . . .
He sang beautiful words, to the spirits from outer space; soundlessly . . .
Everyone on Earth declared that he was mad; obviously . . .
Only privileged souls captured the subtle chords sent by his brain;
                                                            pleadingly . . .

These attuned spirits called to the musician; ceaselessly . . .
'Leave the world of the Earth creatures and join us'; temptingly . . .
'Come and live with us in eternal harmony'; passionately . . .
In a slowly progressive modulation; smoothly . . .
His gifted brain left its unworthy envelope; weightlessly . . .
Playing his rainbow lute in silent melody; *con sordini* . . .
He went on his way to the stars; eagerly . . .

The world never heard the soundless symphony.
                Naturally!

Jacqueline Maire-Greene

Notes

I am 49 and an occupational therapist, running my own busy practice near Geneva, Switzerland, where I have lived for over twenty years, with my husband and two children.

I enjoyed writing poetry as a child and had a poem published at the age of twelve.

Since then, marriage, two children, adapting to another culture and language, and a very busy career have kept pen from paper, but in those rare moments of peace and tranquillity the desire has often returned.

I started writing again in 1996, inspired by a family celebration where I read one of my poems instead of making a speech.

My poems are simply expressions of feelings and emotions, of circumstances involving my life, that of my family and those things around me.

For My Son and His Wife

The bells are pealing in the country church
As I turn to look at you my heart gives such a lurch,
Your smiling face, the face of a boy transformed into a man
Quietly confident to all around, only those close by can see your shaking hand.
Suddenly twenty five years' worth of memories come flooding back to me,
The sleepless nights, your fear of the dark and the wind whistling in the trees,
Your first words, your first painting - we still have it on show,
Your first swing at a golf club struck with such a blow.
The day you and your sister went off to school,
Hand in hand showing her that you're no fool,
You'd protect her from harm and bring her safely home
And you did it all along until she was grown.

Your first day at university, in your room head in hands,
I saw you from the window, it was more than I could stand,
I cried for a week, until I thought stop, that will do
This boy is growing up and I must too!

So here we are in this church, and it's your wedding day,
A father can show the world as he gives his daughter away,
But a mother must hide her sorrow as she hands over her son,
I watch you take her hand, slip on the ring and it's done,
I see my hand there too clasping that of a little boy
Anxiously holding on, wondering have I taught you every ploy,
The image fades and my hand floats away,
It's the back-seat role I now must play.

So it's a whole year down the road, I'm a mother-in-law true,
I know I still nag you both, forgive me if I do,
I've no right to do so, because when I see you together now
It's a couple in harmony, that a year ago made that vow
To be friends, to trust and support each other and that's what you do
Without being afraid of putting forward your own point of view.
You're obviously in love and it's marvellous to see,
We're so proud of you both, keep it up, but be free
Within your relationship to learn to mature and to grow,
And together watch the years move on and harmoniously flow.

Ann McNeil

Holiday 1994
(Majorca)

Notes

I live in Bournemouth, am 71 years old and enjoy writing humorous monologues and poems on current affairs. I scribble monologues for my own enjoyment and for the entertaining of friends.

Publishing success has not been too apparent because it is only recently that I have submitted work for publication.

I wrote my first poem at the age of fourteen, on the Exeter Blitz. I sold the same for threepence a copy for the Baptist Missionary Society.

Perhaps 'twas the aftershave that did it,
The mosquitoes didn't have to think twice.
They were attracted, and then were addicted.
They just loved the smell of *Old Spice*.
They swarmed in and gorged on my body,
With my blood they all had their fill.
Filling themselves up with serum.
In the times when 'twas quiet and still.
To think that I came out from England,
Just to give Spanish *mozzies* a meal.
Paying three hundred quid for the privilege,
Thompsons said it would be a good deal.
I came out with great expectations,
To enjoy both the sea and the sand.
To browse in the shops, read by the pool.
With every mod con near to hand.
The mosquitoes were thrilled with my presence
One could sense they were all overjoyed.
They flew to my flesh with great vigour.
Quite soon they were all well employed.
They soon were my constant companions,
In the bedroom, or out on the beach.
There wasn't one part of my body,
That the perishers didn't try to reach.
I would say that this island is scratchy,
That the Spanish, they should be praised.
As a nation they'd gather a fortune,
On the bumps that their mosquitoes raised.
Me? I'd rather have small English midges.
Those great itchy bumps I don't need.
I was stupid to pay all that money,
Just to give Spanish *mozzies* a feed.

Dennis R Green

The Storm

Notes

I am 40 plus, I work in London, but live in the country. Nature in all its forms fascinates me - especially the wildlife and the power of the elements. This is where most of my inspiration stems from. I have recently started to note down the verses that enter my head.

I am having one other poem published at present, by an American publishing company, entitled *Happy Days!*

Storm clouds race across the sky,
Threatening blackly as they speed on by.

The awesome power of nature holds all in its spell,
As torrential rain lashes hill, valley and fell.

The lightning arcs, forks and blindingly flashes,
The thunder roars, bellows and noisily crashes!

But soon there is calm, and everywhere peace.
It's as if blackness has vanished and all evil has ceased.

Our Creator is victor, good will prevail.
This hope we must cling to, as through life we
travail.

D J Day

Shark!

Notes

I am aged thirty five, married with five children, and have lived in Altrincham (near Manchester) all my life. I am unemployed at the moment. I have been writing poetry since I was nine, although it is only in the last two years that I have sent work in to publishers.

My heroes include C S Lewis, the Brontës, Wordsworth and Dickens. I enjoy history, walking, reading and listening to music.

Shark was written after a sympathetic (to sharks) set of natural history programmes on TV. As you can probably tell, I was not that convinced.

A killer's cold glare pierces through
The salty, sunless waste
Where God in all his mercy had
This demon e're well placed.
Eyes devoid of light and sleep,
Fathomless black pools
Survey a realm of conquest
Where his violence all but rules . . .
For this shadow, stream-lined, long and sleek,
This soaring soul of spite
Kills with all the silent ease
As twilight turns to night.
His throne has no contenders,
No rival here to find,
The only debt to fear the threat
That comes from his own kind
And man, of course, upon whose heart
Not many make a mark
Of blind and frantic terror
Like the presence of a shark.

Anthony Hilton

Notes

Margaret Mary Sherwood is married and has no children.

She has written over 100 poems. She started writing when ill and has never stopped. She takes her inspiration from a spoken phrase, scenery, the weather or seascapes, and writes on waking up - whether in the morning or in the middle of the night.

She sings in her local Methodist choir, enjoys social gatherings, television, videos (travel, nature or classical drama), the theatre, walking, and gardening.

Their Brief Hour

Little, pretty, pure and white;
Pleasures me with such delight;
Glowing like the perfect gem
On the royal diadem.

Sprinkled daint'ly on the grass;
Look up at me when e'er I pass;
A brilliant patchwork is displayed.
By their creator they were made.

When next I saw the flowers fair,
Petals were crushed. The ground lay bare.
It seemed to me so sad a sight.
Such carnage of the crocus bright!

Children bright and true and gay
Went to school one winter's day.
The pride of parent's hope and joy
Was every single girl and boy.

How could they know that their brief hour
Was short as that bright crocus flower.
On schoolroom floor were bodies lain
Of slaughtered children of Dunblane.

Margaret Mary Sherwood

Notes

The New Road

I am a 70 year old housewife from Bangor, County Down, Northern Ireland; I have been writing since I was 12 years old. This is the eleventh poem I have had published, one of which also gained me a Highly Commended certificate in the Scottish Open Poetry Competition of 1977.

The poem printed here was inspired by the desecration caused to the countryside by a new road, built near where I live, and the distress it caused to a dear late friend of mine, Mary Byrne; I would like to dedicate it to her memory. Mary was very upset about the wildlife being chased from their habitat, as was I, and the spoiling of the countryside. Many things inspire my verse - emotions, events or sometimes, just imagination. Writing is my chief hobby, both stories and poetry; I also have one novel written and a second started.

Trees spreadeagled, reaching to the sky,
Bodies inert and twisted where they lie;
What death-throes have they suffered?
Did they die
Silent, resentful, uttering no cry?
Or was there core-deep screaming
Far within
Unheard, unheeded by the slaughterers?

Without mercy, there was meted death
To graceful limbs, now graceless
In demise;
The wind sighs, as with a sobbing breath,
Mourning the passing of the innocents;
Rain drips on sodden earth
From steel-grey skies,
As tears drip from a weeping mother's eyes.

Flora and fauna ravaged in their beds,
Poor remnants these,
That once found shelter from a savage world
Under the spreading green arms
Of the trees;
Now, the land's stripped and naked,
Nothing is left of succour or support,
The needs of modern man
Usurping all;
Bare earth, dead trees, a nothingness
Of desecration like a pall
Laid on the landscape;
Soon, the raw roar
Of traffic will replace the peace
And solitude within whose warm embrace
The wildlife lived secure:

I stare in silence
At the heaped-high sods
And feel the sorrow etched on the earth's face.

Betty McIlroy

The Land of Magic

At 120 mph to the Cotswolds did I fly
My teddy bear and I.

You deserve a few days break
The specialist said -
So I (we) did.

B and B Farmhouse
Eighteenth Century Cotswold stone
Upper Dorey's Cloth Mill
By stream at end of track.

No less than three cats, what joy!
Bobby black as night
White blaze central on face and built-in bib.
Bandaged fourth rear leg, sympathised with me
With only two, requiring stick to make a third.
Still incomplete, said *Bobby*.
Slept on my bed each night.

My good friends, twelve years unseen
To historic houses did drag me,
And to *The Woolpack*
Frequented by the poet, Laurie Lee.

Mine Mill House hosts
Greeted me and waved me on.
I did not want to go -
But literally had
A bleeding heart.

And to the modern Medical Centre, newly built,
Did I fly - just for a check.

MO, said, 'You're a very sick man held
Together, as you say, with parcel tape.'
'Go home, let teddy do most of the driving.'

'Take things easy.'

'That's what I came for,' said I.

But the pain of leaving Painswick and Stroud
Was by far the greater hurt than the heart.

My vow is to return
Again and again and again
(See inscription visitor's book)

I wish now to be buried here
Where I have lived afore -
In another life - déjà vu.

Howard Gaunt

129

Notes

My father was badly gassed in
World War One. He arrived
at the Red Cross Hospital in
Sussex where my mother was
a nurse.

My brother was born in 1918
- he was a Grenadier Guard,
then an officer in the Recon-
naissance Corp. He left Eng-
land January 4th 1943 (my
21st birthday) and was blown
to bits near Tunisia on Febru-
ary 28th 1943.

Remembrance Day

They march in decreasing numbers, medals blazing on their chests
Bent shoulders straightened, heads held higher, eyes turned smartly right
Passed the king's daughter, for whom they gave their best
And the memorial to their comrades, who lost but won their fight.

They were young and gallant, in the prime of life
Proudly following the path their fathers trod three decades before
Unquestioning that this evil could only be solved by strife
Giving five good years, so their sons would fight no more.

They have now grown old, these men who did not die,
Condemned to unfilled promises in a country turning sour,
The land fit for returning heroes, turned out a lie
And all that's left to remember is their finest hour.

Jessie M Leybourne

Notes

I am a 17 year old A level student and live in Bourne-mouth.

I have had two other poems published as a result of competitions, the first being when I was 10 years old, in a local anthology. My interest in po-etry began when I was very little and my mother read poetry to me.

Besides writing my other hobbies are: reading science fiction, drawing and walking in the countryside.

Inspiration for what I write comes from anything and everything.

Untitled

Silences,
In all awkwardness,
Lend themselves to,
Enable thoughts to pass,
Not disturbed by outside,
Conversation at all levels,
Even dust particles halt, in anticipation, of,
Sound.

Kris Dixon (17)

Notes

I am a retired school teacher, married to a retired headmaster. I have two sons, one daughter and seven grandchildren, four of whom are a set of quads.

I began writing poetry soon after my retirement from teaching in 1993, and have work included in more than twenty anthologies published by several different publishers.

I have also had books published: Grannie-Annie's War (memories of my childhood in the second world war) and The Second Decade (memories of my post-war years).

Owl

Briefly
As streaky clouds drift by,
The moon shines through to show
A small white figure perched
On treetop bough on high.

Watching
Through dark nocturnal eye,
The leaf strewn ground below.
The small white figure searched
For woodland creatures, shy.

Silently
A silhouette against the sky.
Unnoticed from below.
Unseen by victim as it reached
The spot where it would die.

Swooping
His wings outstretched to fly,
The hunter swiftly drops down through
The night, to pounce and catch
His prey with piercing cry.

Owl
Flying home across the sky
Seen against the moon's bright glow.
Heard in the night, his ghostly screech
Echoing and fading to a distant sigh.

Anne Crofton Dearle

Notes

At 67, I am married with four children and hordes of grandchildren, who regularly descend on our big house at the seaside, as they all live within fifty miles or so.

I have an MA in Economics and Law from Trinity College, Cambridge, and for sixteen years, prior to my retirement at the age of 55, I was a senior official with the United Nations (ILO and UNIDO: the doing rather than the talking bits).

I lived and worked in the Caribbean for three years, seven years in Africa, four years in Bangladesh and two years in Oman. I have travelled, and still do, on a worldwide basis, our last holiday being to the Karakoram Highway and North West Pakistan.

Much of the poetry I have written has been in a particular context, for example, a game park in Africa or while living in Bangladesh.

Poetry's Fun

Poetry's fun
If the words will run
Off the end of your pen as you're writing.
Even to rhyme
All of the time
Can really be quite exciting!

But to win a prize
That doesn't suffice,
You have to be so esoteric,
Your language impure,
As well as obscure,
And all of your thoughts be *poetic*.

We worship the great
(All of them late)
Poets like Byron and Browning,
But once in a while
We all need to smile,
Not all our expressions be frowning!

Can't we go back
To the rhymes we now lack;
To pondering how many feet are
In every line,
Which isn't a sign,
That the poem has rhythm and metre.

Whoever you meet . . .
Stop a man in the street
And ask him his favourite verses.
I bet that they rhyme,
Have the rhythm and time
Without which modern verses the worse is!

Patrick Davies

Notes

Paula Hewitt has lived and studied in the Middle East and Germany. She worked in historical research and is a fellow of the Huguenot Society, London. She has degrees (Hons) in English language, history and art.

Many of her articles have been published in newspapers and she considers the poetic use of words and language is another challenge.

She greatly admires Dylan Thomas' writing and the Irish female poets of earlier this century, as well as Thomas Hardy.

Paula Hewitt is a new poet who has a lot to say, culled from a very long and interesting life.

Lust

Sitting on top of a double-decker bus,
You look edible, absolutely divine!
I can hardly wait, soon you will be mine!
Hoping to get you home before you sag!
Tentatively I feel you beneath a paper bag!
When at last my lips caress your sugary skin,
I shall experience temptation and mortal sin;
The kitchen table is where it shall be;
In a hurry I'll dispense with formality!
Bare essentials are all we shall need,
Because speed is important if we are to succeed;
I give you a friendly little pinch,
To find you have lost more than an inch;
Yelling to the conductor, I ask him to stop
Quickly onto the platform I manage to drop,
Then my arm is knocked by a clumsy young man,
And my dream is ended as doughnuts get flattened by a Post Office van.

Paula Hewitt

An Ode to Supermarkets

Notes

Consumerism in the 1990's is
food for thought.

*Dedicated to Mark, Lilly and
Daisy.*

Tins and tins of choose-me things,
Standing erect with pride,
Bolder brighter washes whiter
All beckoning me for a trolley ride.

Gradually gradually building up,
Consumer power in each aisle,
Take more than necessities,
The commodities to over-pile.

Sumptuous devilish; pouring sauces,
Starters then main course,
Each brand I hear it shout,
'Take me!'
'No me! To the check-out.'

This one appeared on television,
It must be better than that,
Guiding persuasive advertising,
High nutrition less fat.

Gluttony overwhelms me,
High marketing display,
Items ordered regimentally,
A colourful array.

Is there anything I've missed?
I thumb down the shopping list,
Mmm, no I think it's all here,
As the check-out draws near.

My trolley has a mind of its own,
I look for the shortest queue,
Standing, standing, waiting, waiting,
To push my items through.

The mechanical calculator adds them up,
They come whizzing down at me,
The faceless person at the cash desk,
Demands the appropriate money.

Pay for my future consumption
I receive change with a receipt,
The plastic bags are abstract shapes,
My transaction now complete.

I turn and carry my goods away,
The next person loads their need,
I leave the supermarket behind,
The price to pay to feed.

Anne Armitage

Notes

A British born New Zealand citizen currently living in Nelson, Lancashire, Patricia Checkley, 49, was raised in Malaysia and began writing in her teens.

Her poems are based on personal experiences. *The Interview* is one of them.

Presently employed as a legal secretary, she has in the past worked for an Australian Diplomat, run a Youth Hostel in New Zealand, spent three years in the Merchant Navy as an Assistant Purser and has managed several restaurants with her husband.

Other works, which include a children's epic fantasy and an esoteric novel, all, as yet, remain unpublished.

The Interview

'Come this way,' she said
looking yet not seeing me or
the vast expanse of new carpet
that lay like sprawling grey uncertainty.

'Sit down,' she said
in tones of tolerance, cleverly matching
the sharp angled new wave furniture
the clinical picture frames
the spiked plants
unfolding everywhere.

Scarlet talons clawed through application forms
derisive sniff
'I see you type,' she said
arctic smile she wore all around her frozen lipstick
suffering under sufferance which pissed me off
about the rivalry between those who seek
higher planes
without exception.

Suddenly an overwhelming tiredness took hold
money was necessary
competition superfluous
I'd made a mistake. 'Forget it,'
I said
taking my hope elsewhere.

Patricia A Checkley

Notes

I have lived in the town of Caerphilly all my life and have two children and four grandchildren (both families unfortunately living away from Wales). I will be retiring shortly, from my profession as a Court Welfare Officer (resolving disputes between separating and divorcing couples in respect of contact with, or the residence of, their children).

I started writing, in one form or another, in my teens and since then, I have had several articles (both fiction and non-fiction) published, together with several successes in poetry competitions. My particular interest, however, is in writing poetry and I feel my experience in the social work field has inspired my poetry writing, which is both a therapeutic and cathartic experience. With more time now available, it is my ambition to write an anthology based on social issues, hopefully, involving a mixture of both serious and humorous prose. Furthermore, I would like to set up a writers' circle in my home town.

Apart from writing, I enjoy reading, swimming, walking, theatre and travelling.

My inspiration for this poem came about following a visit to an elderly aunt in a nursing home who, although virtually bed-bound always remained cheerful, constantly reminiscing about the happy times in her life rather than the negative aspects (which I know were many). It was clear that such positive memories were helping her to survive the days and to cope with the trauma of losing her physical facilities.

May Season's Memories Comfort You

So many seasons drift like cobwebbed memories
As long as they last
I am a child again
Nameless pleasures stored deep within
Flood my weary spirit
And in the twilight of my life
     Comfort me.

By candles' flickering glow
Scented rose-filled arbours
Blue-belled carpets and crimson sunsets
     Warm my weakened soul
Soft winds blow softly
     And tell me
All that was . . . still is.

Winter's icy blasts, soft flying flakes
     Float lazily by
Through speckled haze, red raw faces unnamed
     Surface briefly
I reach out to touch
But brittle fingers numbed with pain give up the fight
     And my friends gently fade away.

Bed-bound 'neath white crusted sheets
     I live on long past years
My silent seasonal guests, though bitter-sweet,
     Hold me close
Dissolving senses once more are held at bay
     And in the darkness of the night
          I am at peace again.

Valerie Evans

Notes

My name is Lindsey Jane Colley. I am 15 years old and attend Malet Lambert School in Kingston upon Hull.

I have not been writing poetry for very long - approximately six months. The thing that inspired me the most was a trip to the Lake District with my school, in the summer. We went to study Wordsworth and the wonderful surroundings that inspired him to write poetry and it had the same effect on me.

I was also inspired to write this poem by a diary extract, written by Dorothy Wordsworth (William's sister).

The poem's title simply reflects the scenes of beauty of the Lake District. I enjoy writing poetry and have written more poems in different styles.

When I am not writing poetry, I enjoy listening to music, playing the piano and seeing my friends.

Pure Brilliance

Whilst sitting at the water's edge
Delighted with what I saw
The simplicity of the mountains filled me with such awe
The flowing stream, the dazzling lake the splendour of this sight.
Filled my heart with joy and delight
The old oak trees simply blowing in the breeze
The glossy moss wrapped around the rough bark like a velvet cloak,
Captivating the beauty of that old oak.
The vibrant colours yellows, purples and greens reflecting on those
lavish scenes,

As I walked along the exquisite path,
The cocks were crowing and the people sowing.
It was pure brilliance.

Lindsey Jane Colley (15)

Notes

I have two children, a son and daughter, and three grandchildren. I work as a secretary and live on the Downs in the Wiltshire countryside. I love walking - especially with my dog - and enjoy reading, music, the theatre, craft work, gardening, and doing things on the spur of the moment.

Some time after the end of my twenty nine year old marriage (four years ago), I discovered I could write poetry. The words just came to me; the beauty all around seemed to inspire me. Inspiration comes at night, early morning or when I am out walking.

I wrote *This Day is Mine* after waking up one wet and windy Saturday, wishing I could stay in bed and cancel all my arrangements - when I realised there was nothing to stop me doing just that. I fully appreciated just how precious was each day.

This Day is Mine

A new day dawns,
A new beginning,
This day, I give to you
God said
Use it as you will
The clouds are heavy,
The wind howls,
But, this day is mine

A day of hope
The grass is green,
Rain threatens,
But even so
It's up to me to seize
The wonderful opportunity
That today could bring,
For, this day is mine

In all this darkness,
There is light,
No day is without hope,
I slowly rise and say
My thanks to God
For, this day is mine

I will use it well,
Not waste it in misery
But give praise -
And thanks
That I am free to say
Yes, this day is mine

As I gaze in awe and wonder,
And the enormity of it all
Today will never be again,
It's frightening, exhilarating
But so humbling,
I hug my knees and smile
Yes, this day is mine.

Susan Williams

Notes

I was born in Churchdown, Gloucestershire, in 1951. I am married with four children and four grandchildren. I work as a data co-ordinator and write a weekly column for the Observer Newspaper group, based in Slough.

The poem, *Butterfly Wings*, is taken from a collection called The Circle of Life. The first was written in January 1995; there are over ninety poems in the collection. Two others are being published in anthologies during 1997. There is a personal and spiritual basis to all the poems. My ambition is to see my poetry published as a complete collection.

Butterfly Wings

The wings of a butterfly,
Shimmering in the sun,
Travel the universe,
Unhindered by thought,
A kaleidoscope of colour,
A prism of light,
A rainbow of dreams.
In slow motion,
It floats through,
A fantasy world,
Of orgasmic delight.
Touching the senses,
It colours visions,
Of beauty.
Briefly touching the skin,
Like caressing fingers,
Teasing and taunting,
A lover.
Its breath like,
A gentle kiss,
Fleeting and gone,
Yet it lingers,
Sweet and seductive.
The wings of a butterfly,
So small and fragile,
It has the power,
To move a universe,
With its motion.
Ripples spread through time,
Creating eddies,
So small, yet,
Altering all.

Steve Jones

Notes

This poem was inspired by a dream.

Coronation Postponed

I dreamed last night we were ready for the crowning of a king
We sat, silent and shivering, in a cathedral's massive bowel
Expecting the roar of a thousand voices, for a country's bells to ring
For a land to emerge shining from winter's snowy cowl
And burst, still thawing, into a summer drenched with wine
Giddy with love, trembling beneath dancing, bell-clad feet
When even deep into night the sun would shine
Above the wick of candles and lanterns' moth-enchanting heat
Where couples writhe in the grass, drunk on the scent of each other's hair
On the warmth of each other's cheeks, the addiction of each other's lips
Hands clasped together, wading through syrup-like air
Swimming with pollen, spiralling as warm currents rip
But we sat, hearing only the mournful wind and an echoing creak
As the great doors opened, admitting instead of a king
A whirlwind of bone-dry leaves, instead of a sleek
Golden procession of power, only a scent on the wing
Of a tired breeze, mindful of past summers
Of grass shivering beneath November rain
Only a line of silent mummers
Expressive faces creased in pain
And yet we sit in the dark
And wait still.

Laurence Cole

Notes

I almost stumbled into the world of poetry eighteen months ago. I responded to an invitation from Forward Press, for new poets to submit a poem. Since its acceptance, poetry has been a source of surprise and delight; I have now had quite a few poems in anthologies and three magazines.

Nature gives me great joy and inspiration and this poem was written when I was ill and confined indoors. I felt sad I couldn't see the seasonal beauty first hand and remembered the wild violets I had recently photographed. At least I had my photographs.

Spring Snaps

Purple spots among the green,
they're here again.
Newly washed by fresh spring rain
just down the lane.

You have to step off the path
and search for them;
Tiny blooms on slender stems,
each one a gem.

Beneath shady undergrowth
they lowly lie,
Missed by unobservant eye
too quick, pass by.

With modesty they arrive,
their month is May.
When they've served their short-lived day,
they slip away.

They're like little princesses
in purple gowns,
Dainty heads bob up and down,
deserving crowns.

I used to love the cool air,
so fresh and clean,
Spring came bursting on the scene
and brushed me green.

Now I can't get down the lane,
and so I look
At violets in my book
of snaps I took.

Mary Care

Notes

I am in my mid-fifties, married, and have two dogs, Charlie and Becky. I work part-time as a telephonist/receptionist.

I have had one other poem published. My hobbies include collecting books and rummaging at car boot sales. I began writing poetry as a girl, but did not keep any until about twenty years ago, and only submitted some for publication recently.

This poem was written during a period when my life was going through many changes. Reading it now reminds me how much my life has changed.

Self

Who am I an empty shell a chrysalis wherein I dwell
a mind without the knowing.

Mute of mouth and blind of eye facing inwardly I lie
a child but for the growing.

Here within my self-made womb I ignore the voice of doom
heedless of its crying.

In my darkness I survive selfish dreams I keep alive
while the world is dying.

Barbara Robinson

Isn't it Lovely in the Sunshine

Notes

I retired in 1984, after working as a hospital theatre technician. I started writing poetry after my wife's death, in September, 1990.

One of my poems, *Creation*, was published in Poetry Now - South 1993.

This new poem was composed to recall a treasured moment. Etched on my mind are the few words of my dearly loved wife, Olivia, during a final walk on a lovely sunny Sunday, in September, 1990. Pushing her wheelchair, we stopped to rest before returning home. She quietly remarked to my daughter and I, 'Isn't it lovely in the sunshine.'

I dedicate this poem to my life's love - Olivia.

What can you feel with sky so clear
Warm rays enfold and seep into your soul.
A balm to weary senses.
It lights the spider gossamer after rain,
Drops beading round the fragile frames.
Like prisms casting light in all directions
The pearly lobes of dew full stretching down,
The maker's strength to test.

Child skips, and laughs, through sunny day.
The weary lift their hearts to snatch its joy
And say - 'Isn't it lovely in the sunshine.'
But then we look - and sky has clouds,
Moved by a freshly wind round earth,
An ever-changing ceiling to life's room.
No sense can dull with any sameness
A kaleidoscope in time, glow and gleam
Then change,
With halo setting golden lamp sinks down
Ablaze with pink and yellow gowned.
It frames the lowing clouds bright edge on dark.
To move where other dwellers rise and greet
Its warming arch for day anew - with praise,
And say - 'Isn't it lovely in the sunshine.'

Charles F Williams

Notes

I would like to dedicate this poem to my dear mother, Olive.

Park Seat

Just a seat painted green
In the park, amongst a scene,
Of quiet beauty -
Familiar things, a seat,
Of magic moments.

So many times we settled there,
On summer days - the sunshine shared -
We knew the trees,
Their shape, and form -
The squirrels, birds, and life adorned.

I sit there now
It's not the same
A single dove flew down and came,
Quite close to me, and,
Caught my eye - its studied look,
I'll not deny, a fascination.
So strange it looked - then,
Walked away - looked back awhile,
As if to say - 'I know why you are sitting there,'
Then gently took to wing - and air,
With grace, above me.

Nicholas Lesley

Notes

Shelagh Skinnard is a semi professional soprano. She is a housewife living in Cornwall, married to a lawyer and with one daughter, Bethany, plus sundry horses, dogs, geese, hens and other animals.

She started writing poetry when in her late forties, about four years ago. Simple incidents of everyday life can trigger off an idea for a poem.

Lovers

They were smug as lovers sitting in restaurants
watching the others
That couple is married they thought aloud
we will never be as them they silently vowed
Then they married, the years quickly passed
They still eat in restaurants
with eyes on their glass
A companionable silence
That's what it's called
Kidding themselves love hasn't palled.

Shelagh Skinnard

The Old Mulberry Tree

Notes

After having spent all my life in the caring profession, it did not allow much time for hobbies! Especially as I am happily married to a wonderful husband and we have a lovely daughter. Life has been hectic at times, not to mention very hard work.

When I retired three years ago, I vowed to do what I dreamed of all my life - here was my chance - to write. I had never read any poetry in my life - still don't. I tried and found it very therapeutic, reflective and exciting. It is a way to express all my lifetime of stored memories.

I only write what I feel, from the heart. It is a challenge to find acceptable expressions which convey those events to you, the reader.

Besides my new-found hobby, I love gardening, cooking, nature, family life and meeting people.

All that is left to dream of now, is the day when my own volume of my life's treasures will appear in print, to be shared by all poetry readers.

I dedicate this poem to my dear husband, Robert, a pillar of strength for the past thirty three years - with heartfelt thanks and love, always.

If only, I could be there again,
Dreaming, while plaiting a daisy chain!
In the shade of that old mulberry tree,
Oh so long ago, now only a vague memory.

Steamy summer days, were spent dreaming
Watching the swallows fly low,
In the distance, children screaming!
The luscious meadow, a shimmering green glow.
Dotted with daisies, buttercups, a beautiful scene,
Muffled cow-bells in the distance, oh so serene!

That old tree, stood proud up high,
On a river-bank, as if to pierce the sky!
The great Danube River, gracefully flowing with its tide,
Quietly, meandering through slumbering countryside!

Steamy, balmy summer days, were spent idling time away,
Sheltering, in the shade, watch the pink flamingo wade.
Through the mud-flats, uphill, on the meadow to graze,
Their daily fill, as time almost stood still!

On the river, sailing yachts passing each other
Lazily stirring the water, causing it to ripple,
Exchanging greetings and the odd tipple!

I often wonder, if that old tree still stands,
On the beautiful River Danube banks?
So gracefully giving shelter and shade,
To any passing stranger, dare to invade,
To rest on long hot summer days, in that cool shade!

Listening to the frogs croak and the reeds sway!
Where swans are leaping, causing a splash,
Competing for their daily catch!
Swallow darting, flamingos wade,
And the nightingale sings, under the mulberry shade!

That, a most wonderfully, serene place on earth,
A memory, forever treasured, deep in my heart.

A Elliott

Notes

I am 15 years old. A year 11 GCSE student, working part-time as a waitress. I live in Leek, Staffordshire, with my Mum, Dad, two brothers, four ducks, two ferrets and a cat named 'Bagpuss'.

My hobbies include anything connected with art. I enjoy my elocution lessons where I read and learn poetry for my examinations in speech and drama.

One night I sat down and began to think back to when I was a child and of what happened on Hallowe'en. This gave me the inspiration for my poem. The poem describes that particular night.

I am lucky to have parents who support me in all my interests.

Hallowe'en

'Knock knock, who's there?' I say
It's monsters standing on my bay.
Trick or treat they ask
As they come under cover from their mask,
I give them a treat, a fun-size Mars
If I didn't, foam would be on the cars.
Yes, it's Hallowe'en
Yes, I said, I've seen.
'Oh no!' the children shout
While the witches are about.
Already the skies are dark
Until the pumpkins begin to spark.

Esta Stubbs

Shirl Grows Up

Come on out, Shirl.
>Where are you going?

Up the town centre;
Have us some fun.
>Everything's shut now.
>It's nearly midnight.

Aw, come on out, Shirl,
Come along out, Shirl;
Let's have some fun.

>Just walk around there?
>Boring, that's boring.
>I've had enough. I'm going to bed.

(I cross my fingers: listen, listen.)
Shirl slams the door; looks in at the kitchen.
'Night, Mum,' and stomps upstairs.
I sigh, thankful. Outside, they're shouting:

Aw, come on out, Shirl;
Don't be so wet.

(Go away, go away,
You'll wake the neighbours.)
Shirl just ignores them.
Hold my breath; crash!
That's the gate slammed.
Voices and footsteps
Fade away, fade away,
Towards the town centre.

Next morning's radio;
Local news; Last night
A gang of young teenagers,
Some girls only thirteen
Caught in the town centre
Smashing shop windows,
Looting parked cars.

Shirl listens silent,
Sipping her coffee.
Stares a long time
At the window, at nothing.

You going out, Shirl?
She thinks before answering.

>No, Mum, I'm busy.
>I've got lots of homework.

F Jones

149

Notes

I am 52 and have a son, Kevin, who is 30. I am an ex-secretary and live in Cross-ford, by Dunfermline.

I have had three poems published. I like reading, country walking, cycling and swimming.

My husband, Douglas, has been ill for many years with ME and has been confined to the home. It's only in the last year that he has been able to get around. In 1995, we had a holiday in Crail, the first time for years. We were sitting at the harbour one day, enjoying it, and that's what inspired the *Crail* poem - appreciation after many years housebound.

It is dedicated to my husband, Douglas and son, Kevin, who both have a sense of humour which has kept us going through the bad days.

Crail

The harbour was busy,
artists painting,
seagulls soaring,
the sea lapping the shore,
people laughing, children playing,
it's a joy to sit and absorb
all of life on a summer's day,
on up to the pottery to choose a bowl,
a little family business with soul,
so many to see, it's hard to decide,
I'll sit awhile and have a think
and chat to folk as they pass by,
the sun dapples through the trees
and shines on all the creations
it's lovely to sit on the bench in the sun.
How artistic some people are.

Linda Matheson

Notes

Out of work because of illness, I am 55 years old and have five children, all grown up. I was born, and have lived, in Cardiff all my life. I love the whole of Wales, its culture and people; the sad part is that parts of Wales were no better off than the third world. When working, I was a manager for a national food company.

Most things in life interest me; I enjoy the paper work which I do for a local club. I also enjoy all sport in general. The people I love are very special to me.

My first poem took me six months to write, I used up a full pad, couldn't get it to work out. Then it came to me - I called it *My Wales*. It was published by Poetry Now - I was really pleased with myself.

Starting in 1994, twenty four of my poems have been published since then. I have a dream of writing my own book, and have also written a couple of short stories.

I am inspired to write by this Government and what it's done to Wales. I put my thoughts in writing and call them the Hyena and Tarzan, but my poetry verse covers a variety of topics.

The Wind

Dawn breaking over the mountain wall a cold clear morning
no artificial light, violent burst of wind blurred vision for
flying birds, landslide in front of their eyes.

The birds desperate their powerful wings making no headway,
no system to overcome the violent wind, an adventure turning
into an impossible mission.

Exhausted whizzed backwards blown off course illuminated sky.
The only audience the eagle lurking on the wind, no lengthy trip
for him, an outcast flying in the sky.

The violent wind breaking open the clouds the closed feathers of
the eagle staring down, the estuary sleeping a warm wet wind the
incoming sea white lip waves turning into choppy waters, throbbing
noise the divorced wind like a roller-coaster no scruples.

Wind of fear ripping the sea wall apart huge waves driven on by
swirling winds, debris covering the estuary floor sea waves like
a volcano erupting white spray like a jigsaw falling on the
crumble sea floor.

A homeless wood broken apart shivering leaves jagged trunks
branches lying naked on the carpet of dead leaves, then silence
The violent wind blowing itself out nature's sleepy eyes no role
to play, the violent wind destroys this day, nature's rebirth will
have its day.

Garrett John

As My Shadow Fades

Notes

I started writing poetry ear-
lier this year (1996). I used it
as a form of relief from
studying for my GCSE's! *As
My Shadow Fades* describes
someone's thoughts at a cer-
tain stage in life. The last two
lines are the most important
to me but they are also
quite enigmatic. The shadow
should be considered as one's
past. If one disregards one's
past that is when one starts to
ebb away.

Is there anyone there who knows?
How to silence my endless woe.
Is there anyone there who cares?
Long enough to whisper a prayer.

Where will my river flow?
Killing the banks where nothing grows.
My mind's displaced an empty heart,
Please, just tell me what's on my cards.

I'll try to stop the fiend inside,
I'll rise above, strong as the tide,
But when will I ebb away?
Maybe when my shadow fades.

Esha Dasgupta

Notes

Iris Kemlo is a married civil servant from Hampshire, with two grown-up children and a supportive husband. She started writing poetry to remember holidays, about ten years ago, mainly to amuse family and friends.

She is one of the founder members of St Vincent Singers, a choir of parents who sing for charity at old people's homes and hospitals in the area. She has had a few poems published in local magazines.

The Coming of Spring

The land it is awakening, spring comes back to the earth
The snowdrops raise their dainty heads, bob up and down in mirth,
The buds transform the barren trees and birds rebuild their nests,
The children watch the frog-spawn grow in the pool's dark muddy depths.

The daylight slowly lengthens as winter leaves the land,
The gardeners get out their tools, the lawns get out of hand,
They plant the seeds for summer, for vegetables and for flowers,
The weeds will soon be cleared away before April's many showers.

The daffodils are next to show a splash of colour bright,
On roundabouts and roadside kerbs they are a pleasant sight.
Now all we wait for are the lambs to frolic in the fields,
Kicking up their spindly legs as winter to springtime yields.

Iris Kemlo

Notes

I am a 71 year old widow, living in Surrey with my 19 year old grandson and my cats. My main interests are writing, reading, gardening, painting and environmental issues.

I have been scribbling away since the age of 15, but I've only recently started submitting poetry for publication. This poem is the fifth to be published in eighteen months - very satisfying.

When the Sea Empress disaster happened I felt more could have been done to avert it. I was so angry that my poem literally burst out of me - just as the oil did from the tanker!

Oil Tanker Disaster

No - not again!
Once more we see
The fruits of man's stupidity.
The thoughtlessness
And endless greed,
The lives of which we take no heed.
Cargoes of death
On rust-bucket ships,
That are only fit for rubbish tips.
Need we ask why?
We have before.
When we find dying on our shore,
Some poor creature
That's meant to be
In its natural home, the sea.
We know the cause
And the solution
Put an end to all pollution.
The sea is not
A bottomless bin
For us to throw our discards in.
God meant this world
For all to share,
Trusted his creatures to our care.
Let's have more thought
Every nation.
Show them more consideration.
Don't take so much,
Do more giving.
That's the way we should be living.

Daphne Lodge

Notes

This poem is dedicated to Derek.

The idea for it came whilst visiting my husband in hospital.

Nemesis

He dwells within an empty brain,
His speechless voice can call no name.
He lies within a shattered soul,
Lost knowledge will not make him whole.

He dwells beneath an unborn face,
Caricature of the human race.
He lies within a grotesque form,
From which all being has been torn.

He dwells within a world within,
Oblivious of time, of sin.
He lies within a silent head
Where silent voices raise the dead.

He dwells behind unseeing eyes
Seeping tears that won't disguise.
He lies beneath his cold white sheet,
And figures come, to keep him neat.

He dwells within a wounded mind
Which thought and reason cannot bind.
He lives within an altered state,
A savage muse has sealed his fate.

He lies within his flaccid frame,
A sediment of some vast game.
His imprint fills an empty space,
He is condemned. In time. In place.

Maureen Lenihan

Notes

I have been writing poetry for just one year, as a means of filling my time and exercising my intellect, since poor health prevents my working.

I wrote *The Night* at the request of my local poetry circle, who set the length and subject matter of the poem. I completed it in about two days and it was read out at the poetry circle by a friend.

The Night

As dusk and dark start to descend,
And weary workers homeward wend,
The pipistrelle, though nearly blind,
Its way through gath'ring gloom will find.

The night descends on weary town,
Dressing it in nature's gown
Of velvet black with spangled light,
Setting off the moon's pale white.

The darkling night with stars arrayed,
Its velvet beauty all displayed
With brightly glowing, twinkling light,
A show put on for man's delight.

Hedgehogs round the garden shuffle,
Seeking food with sniff and snuffle,
And nightjars churr throughout the night,
While owls float by in muffled flight.

The rodents, such as mice and voles,
Must leave the safety of their holes,
And forage for their nightly food,
Returning safely to their brood.

The clock strikes twelve with ringing bell,
Releasing nightmares straight from hell,
With demon, goblin, elf and sprite,
Causing mayhem, shock and fright.

Then man lies cringing in his bed,
And night is given to the dead,
The ghosts and ghoulies stalk abroad,
Their supernat'ral rule assured.

The nascent sun foretells the morn,
And darkness ends; night's mantle torn,
Brings light on which all life depends,
Until once more the night descends.

D R Mason

Notes

The poem was written above the clouds on a plane between South Africa and England, prompted by an overwhelming feeling of isolation and aloneness. All I was in control of at that point were my thoughts.

Now 24 years old, I have travelled like a nomad for the last six years, around the time I first started writing.

Putting my thoughts to paper, not just as poetry, is my way of struggling with the demons of everyday and future life, while trying to relinquish the grip of my past.

Reflections

Mirror can you see what I cannot
See inside of me?
And tell me the truth, if I'm like you,
A deaf and blind mute.
You never lie, though hard you try
To be as fair as ever.
But hide you can't, the outer glance
That belies the troubled sinner.

The pain I feel, you cannot heal
Your emotions are not real.
A smile, a tear, a laugh
All but stir an indifferent heart.

Nicholas Stevens

Notes

I was born 6th March 1954 in Luton, where I still live, and work as a manufacturing operator for a local car firm. I have been married twice.

I have been writing poetry for about twenty years and first presented one for publication in November 1995. Since then, I have had eight poems published in anthologies. I have also submitted one to the National Museum of Scotland to celebrate its opening in 1998. My inspiration comes from inner emotions on a variety of subjects.

After so many years of reading, seeing photographs and films, I felt the need to express that war is not glory to celebrate, but human tragedy that follows. The remains of war are forgotten all over the world, small wars as well as the published ones.

War Leftovers

They are children of despair
Their lives beyond repair
Diseased and forgotten
Left and downtrodden
In misery they live
Germs around them thrive
These are the remains of wars
Bodies covered in sores
Desperate and emancipated
Hair all matted
Dirty and lost
This is the war cost
Left to die
Wherever they lie
Is this the reward for war?
If so, let's have no more.

Malcolm W Davison

Notes

My full name is Derek Shaw; I sign all my poems 'Derek'. I live in Rossendale, Lancashire, and am married to Lynne: we have three children and four grandchildren.

This is the second poem I have had published by Poetry Today, and I have also had other work published. I am a new poet, but I have already written a collection of poems based on a comedy character I have created. It is now my ambition to see my three volumes published.

Last, but not least, I hope to complete my hat trick and have a third poem published in Poetry Today's next book.

Special Offers

I really do like shopping
I told the wife it's fun
Especially when we pass a shop
I think that I have won.

But then she sees that magic sign
The Sale in big bold print,
I know quite well when we go in
It's going to cost a mint.

Then when we get to ladies' wear
I just know what she will say,
'Look at this it's really cheap
I'll buy it for a rainy day.'

But one thing I have learnt
Is never to disagree,
'Cause if I do, I know what's next
She'll go off and buy three.

Next it's down to underwear
I saw her eyes light up.
Because she saw this wonder bra
In a 36B cup.

'Look,' she said, 'They've pants to match
Do you think I could have these,
I could wear them for my birthday'
Then she gave my hand a squeeze.

There I was with all these bags
But I know there's more to come,
So I suggest I wait outside
And meet her when she's done.

There I was on my own
Looking all sad and glum,
Because you know I've changed my mind
Shopping ain't much fun.

Derek

159

Notes

The dancer was a beautiful young Indian girl from Madras, at the start of her career, who I met on my visit to India.

The Indian Dancer

Dance my little Gopi - dance
The temple dance of Krishna,
Beat, insistent drummer beat
The Pantheon beat of Shiva.

Come, my little milkmaid come,
The stage is set and waiting -
Come in red and glittering gold,
Your devotees submitting.

Coil that tiny form to right,
To left - a cobra coiling.
Stretch that neck to be a swan,
With pride - a peacock splaying.

Stamp your feet to stir the bells -
The ankle bells you're wearing,
Let the rhythm of the drum,
Set the heart-beats throbbing.

Move your tiny hands up high,
Then your eyes will follow.
Jet black eyes and ruby lips
Make the God-head callow.

Now the eyes control the mind,
The mind, a mood en-nobling -
Mood is moved to sentiment,
And sentiment is loving.

Pose, my lovely lotus pose,
With open petals gleaming -
Mimic all the beauteous things,
And set the wide world dreaming.

So dance, my little Gopi dance -
You're now the bride of Krishna.
Beat, beloved heart, become
The wonder of the Sastra.

Elizabeth Blackbourn

Notes

I am a housewife and mother. My son died aged 2 years and eleven months, on the 2 December 1967. I have never been able to write about him until now. I have two daughters, aged 34 years and 18 years.

My hobbies are reading, gardening and religious matters, mostly. I started writing in school where I had a dedicated teacher. I have been writing for many years, mostly in Welsh, and am usually inspired by circumstances around me.

This poem was written for my little boy, who had a very cruel disease. I felt very alone during this sad time and have always felt my grief was mine alone.

It is dedicated to my son, Dewi Wyn, and yes I do still love him. He will always be a cherished child for me, and the world has not touched him. He is still as pure as the white snowflakes which covered his grave for weeks after the funeral. The flowers were intact when the thaw came three weeks later. They stayed like that for many more weeks in the middle of a harsh cold winter. Thus the line: 'Trying to beautify the harsh earth'.

My Son ~ Dewi Wyn

You were born
On a thunderous day,
The clouds were hanging
Heavily in the sky.

You were pressed
A small warm bundle
Into my arms.
And then I vowed
To love you
Forever.

Death hung over you
Cold and calculating;
Rummaging through your tiny body
Ravaging your beauty.
And finally
It won.

The snowflakes
Fell with quiet ease;
Covering your grave
So white and pure.
The flowers
Colourful.
Trying to beautify
The harsh earth.

And there I stood
Alone in my grief.
Vowing to love you
Forever.

Dilys Baker

Notes

M Taylor Thomson lives in Aberdeen. Although she has had work published in connection with her past employment in press and publicity, only recently, since her retirement, has she concentrated more time to poetry.

Her poem is an allegory of humanity's constant search to find the meaning and source of life - *The Fountain of Love*. She believes the universe was conceived in love by the Creator, so that life would evolve to become human and, eventually, know love and be able to treat each other and creatures with kindness.

The Fountain of Love

Bring me the white mountain of
    the solitude; remote from the
    city's noisy crowds.
Leave me on the crest of its highest
    peak so I can find if you're
    hiding in its shrouds.

Gently, place me on the wide white
    river and carry me kindly down
    to the sea.
Let me search the sunken caves for
    your secrets. I'll keep faith
    whilst looking for thee.

Fly me on the wild night winds of
    adventure, far beyond the gold
    moon up above.
Deep, deep into outer space let me
    travel until I reach
        You
    The Fountain of Love.

M Taylor Thomson

Belief

You say there's no Creator? Then come along with me
And see the flowers, the trees, the streams
And watch the sunlight's dancing beams
And hear the birds or smell a rose
Then tell me, 'Who created those?'
I'd like to know how you explain
The warming sun, the cooling rain
The stars that light the night time sky?
Such wondrous things. It makes me sigh to hear you say
'There is no God. I don't believe.'
I'm sad for you. It makes me grieve
Your eyes don't *see*. Your ears don't *hear*
The truth that's all around
To touch, or see, or listen to
For when you do you've found
Your soul has been awakened, you look with clearer eyes
Your ears tune in to purer sound
You breathe the air and touch a leaf.
Yes, God is real . . . you've found *belief.*

Dorothy Mason

Waiting

Night and day,
       And you're waiting.
You don't know what you're waiting for.
Unaware, time slipping by,
Life going on as before.

Until, one day, you're counting hours,
And death's coming in at your door.
Now, you know what you're waiting for.

Pettr Manson-Herrod

Notes

I am 74 years old and retired, a widower with one son. I live in Malvern, Worcestershire.

The environment is of interest to me but my main hobbies are music and poetry.

Latterly I have come to realise that without water and sunshine there wouldn't be any clouds; no life.

I have had my poems *The Worcestershire Beacon* published in Poetry Now (Central) 1992 and *Eccentric Evolution* in Poetry Now (With Tongue in Cheek) 1994.

Clouds

High in the heavens, soaked up by the sun,
The sustainers of life their journey's begun;
So high, so beautiful this glorious day,
Menacing, foreboding when storm's on the way.

Borne by the winds that blow 'cross the seas,
Hastened and chastened and sometimes at peace.
Herein lie the rivers, the lakes and the streams,
Here too lie our lives, our hopes and our dreams.

From the heavens above come support for the bees,
All creatures that breathe, the shrubs and the trees,
The beautiful flowers, the grass in the field;
Without clouds to death all life must yield.

Raymond Morris

Fire of Red

Shimmering and glowing,
copper-ball of fire,
alighting the sky,
as a carpet of golden red haze.
Tranquilly - gliding,
swiftly, swirling,
emerging as a brilliant flame a-shimmering
nestling on the distantly bound horizon.
Just awaiting nature's - camouflage -
of autumn leaves and trees,
gently forming patterns,
a-fluttering in the breeze,
such beauty profounds itself
and belies belief.

Jane Sander

Family History

Searching for names
Of others gone before
Looking for the evidence
Of what you stood for.
Finding records
Connecting links
Stories of work
Flow once again.
Pictures of places
Of people too
From Saxon invasion
To Victorian times.
In libraries,
Galleries and
Church
All come together
Pieces of history
Alive and present
In my time.

Lilian Louise McGuckien

Notes

I wrote this poem to cheer up my Nan who had gone into Clatterbridge Hospital, Wirral. She made me laugh as Mum said she wouldn't go into hospital that morning until she had finished the Guy Fawkes. It was left for me and my brother, Ashley, when we came home from school.

I would like to dedicate this poem to all the doctors and nurses who have helped our Nan, Irene Beddard, to keep going even though she has lung cancer.

My Nan

My Nan is very special to me
She makes my breakfast
and makes my tea
My Nan is very special you see
she shouts at my mum
if she shouts at me.

She never comments when I am bad
she just says 'Byron I'll tell your dad'

My Nan is very clever you know
she can cook, clean and sew
she made a Guy Fawkes for me today
that's just one thing
what else can I say.

My Nan is as brave as brave can be
she goes for chemotherapy
then comes home tired and hot,
but helps with my homework
yes she does the lot,
gives me a hug, never complains
my Nan I love
and that remains.

Byron Houghton (10)

Notes

Douglas Campbell, 23, lives in Strathaven, Scotland. A very active mountaineer, he has climbed extensively the world over.

He uses poetry as a medium through which he can convey the intensity of feeling experienced whilst in the mountains.

The inspiration for this poem was the Svaebreen Glacier in Arctic Svalbard, beside which the poet spent an unforgettable night watching icebergs calve into the sea.

The poem is dedicated to the memory of his great friend, Stuart Adam. Stuart was beside Douglas on that wonderful night, but died in a climbing accident on 26th January 1991, in Glen Clova, Scotland.

The 'Bergs of Svaebreen

Towers of shadow, glinting white
Hanging, poised on sea, ice-bright

Tinkle, crackle, groan and crash
And I, just me with tonnes of clear sea

It hallows all, and down to earth
I tumble, humbled; without a breath

No understanding the mirrors of power
Which glimmer, shimmer in our great hour

I walk along the ice-strewn shore
On judgement day, like drugs need more

The deep, dark distance flecked with white
The slight orange sky, a trapper's delight

Sudden, and loud, with rush of air
The silence is broken and déjà despair

Framed in my mind, the picture is clear
The waves and the shore will truly be dear

In years to come, our time gone by
In a small glass jar, close to my eye . . .

Douglas Campbell

Notes

I am a married man with two boys, aged five and seven. I was born in Crumpsall, Manchester, in 1966. I work for Social Services and have lived in Chadderton for eight years. I am currently writing a book about a young boy and his relationships and concerns, through adolescence.

I am a keen golfer and I only started to write poetry after an operation, which sidelined me for five months. This poem is one of about one hundred I have penned.

Whale of a Time

The night's black and silent, the ocean sits still,
There's just a slight breeze sending ripples at will,
I sit and I wait for I know he'll arrive,
I know that he's here and he'll jump and he'll dive.
As if he has heard me, he lifts through the sea,
He's large as a mountain and blue and so free,
He leaps and he sprays and he crashes back down.
He spins round the moon - he's a big dancing clown.
It seems to be over, at least for tonight,
His singing dies down and my friend's out of sight.

M G King

Notes

I was born in 1920 and married twice. I have four children and five grandchildren. Now retired from work as an area technical representative for an international engineering company, I live in Chinnor, Oxfordshire.

I have written many poems and short stories, a few have been published but no outstanding awards or prizes. I've always enjoyed writing humorous scripts for variety shows in which I have been involved.

I am interested in my children and grandchildren, friends and people generally. I enjoy writing, drawing, reading, music and DIY. My sports were rugby, tennis and swimming, mainly.

People, their behaviour and personalities inspire me. Years spent in the Western Desert and South Africa inspired this poem, *Nightfall*.

Nightfall

A cool breeze fans the sun-dried flowers and trees.
They lift their drooping heads as if refreshed;
As traveller a heart'ning mirage sees,
Whose faded soul revives with dreams of rest.
A sudden stillness falls upon this barren land.
A brooding silence that can 'most be felt.
As angry waves cease roaring when they reach the land,
Or close of tropic rains upon the veldt.
The trees and flowers display a diff'rent face;
Released at last from sun's undying light.
Once more refreshed, they're freed to take their place
To join the magic charm of fall of night.

P T Charles

Notes

Aged 73 years, I retired in
1983 after fifteen years
teaching. I was born in Bir-
mingham and educated at
King Edward VI Grammar
School.

My interests are art, music
and the countryside. Writing
became a personal exercise
only, helping me to face the
future after the loss of my
partner in 1980. I have no
previous publications.

Memories

Dreaming dreams of days gone by,
Pictures of the past returning,
Actions, words, all in their setting
As if 'twere only yesterday.
Like the old magic lantern
The mind clicks over frame to frame,
Loved ones re-emerge and smile,
Absent friends briefly return.
Better than any tale of fiction
Is our own book of life
To turn the pages at our will,
Our own recorded history.

Edna Wright

Notes

I was born in Liverpool at Easter, 1929, and attended Queen Mary High School. I worked as an insurance clerk in Liverpool. I'm married with five children and ten grandchildren, and have lived in Winsford for twenty one years.

My poems have been published by Anchor Books and Arrival Press, of Peterborough, and another has won a third prize in the Other Side of the Mirror, by The International Society of Poets. Another is to be published by Poetry in Print this year.

My interests include reading, writing, crosswords, word wheels, gardening, knitting, embroidery and tapestry.

I have been writing poetry for four years, at first during the early hours, when suffering from insomnia. I attend a creative writing course.

I have strong feelings about factory farming; intensive farming methods horrify me. I am sensitive to the suffering of others. I have had poems about victims of war and victims of violence published.

Factory Farming

A hell on earth to be their fate
the sow in a stall and calf in its crate,
commodities all with a price on each head
in this high tech food chain farm animals tread.
No fresh cool air or gentle summer rain
just the allotted space, mere mortals ordain.
No seasons here, all falsely endowed
for tiers of hens complaining shrill and loud.
Eggs laid to schedule, a production line,
poultry imprisoned in their cells *doing time.*
A feathered conveyor belt *until death do part*
designed strictly for profit, no feeling no heart.

Sheelagh Evans

Notes

Born 11th November 1910, an only child, in Southampton. Worked first as a children's nurse then during the war on munitions. Afterwards became a civil servant in Watford.

My hobbies include: painting, writing stories and poems and I'm passionately fond of cats.

Twilight Hour

What is beauty? Is it something more
than just a few Miss Worlds that hold the floor,
or fashion conscious models in a book.

With thrusting limbs and staring, icy, look.
Perhaps these other things have value too -
a rosebud bathed in early morning dew,
a bird upon the wing,
the purple clouds of lilac in the spring.

Where is beauty now? Will it be sought,
as concrete jungles rise to cleave the sky,
and man-made monsters tear the earth apart,
and rivers die.
Poisonous weapons flung into the void,
all in the name of peace, the earth defiled,
and radioactive dust contaminates
the helpless human race, the unborn child.

The young are wretched, what is there for them?
They see no hope of any future years.
Born in the shadow of the bomb
and bred in a darkening world,
they fall beneath the weight of all their fears.
They lose the battle, though they fight.
Armed with the needle and the drug,
they drift into a world of endless night.

The world grows old, but once men had a dream,
and knights rode forth upon their valiant steeds
to banish wrong, and to defend the right.
Sleepers awake, the evil day is seen,
for where is beauty now, and where the dream?

J M Terry

Notes

The less worldly have always maintained that the late King George V always said 'Book Bognor', immediately before he died in 1935.

A retired Anglican priest, formerly vicar of Chipping Campden in Gloucestershire, Peter J Millam's ministry is now that of the poetic word.

Copyright of his hymn, O They That Go to Sea in Ships, now rests with the Missions to Seamen and was sung on Sunday Half Hour (Radio 2) on Sea Sunday, 14th July 1996, and in many churches and cathedrals that day.

Book Bognor

'Bugger Bognor!' gasped the King.
Then he did the decent thing
And died upon the palace bed,
Nevermore to lift his head.
Come the Day of Judgement, when
Deeds, words and thoughts of men
Are laid bare for all to see;
There the King will make his plea:
'*Bugger* never passed my lips.
The word is really your own quips.
What I said, which you mistook,
Was, 'O yes! Bognor please do book.'

Peter J Millam

Notes

This poem is inspired by the multitude of atrocities that have visited people throughout history, and the loss of culture and knowledge that follows.

As a whole, several words are contrived, with the intention that the reader is aware of how they are caused to feel, rather that arriving at specific definitions.

Deast: a person or people not yet dead, but having a life of such misery and suffering that death is no release.

Wonnle: surrender and retreat without honour, pride or dignity.

Smy: when a person, or people, is degraded though they were once great.

Dead are the Deast

Glutterwups rise in sorty hordes
    seeking gainly trays
    Shunnies defer into fraining frays
'Oh let us wonnle' they sply and cry
    'oh let us wonnle, not have us die'
But Glutterwups are gainly greedy in their gnashing way
    and so abund to kill and syphon Shunnies, Fwinnies
    and Boocks alike
Now the ground is clast with worming blood of the deast
    and the sky is blask with the charred colour of the deast
    timeless towers are bond and burned
'I am 'fraid' cry the carroned child
'I am rapt' cry the mirthing mother
'I am brock' cry the paining papa
But Glutterwups have greedy grins in the din
    and do not defer continued rapturous culling
With grunty steaming hearts
    from the crucible of their ocred souls
    with bane acid intent and dire buried vision
    forlorn the clawed grapping
    the wet skinning, pinning and prune
In suffer the deast clasping bonded hands pray to die
    pray be it soon
No longer will be the recoiled silent Fwinnies
    the page ancestry will be dork and smy
    the old said wise ones will be crooned and dry
The deast have ended
    have ended the deast.

Richard Pierre Reid

Notes

I am a housewife, mother and grandmother. I have had a few childhood memories and poems published.

From a child, my love of animals has resulted in my taking in, and caring for, many sick domestic and wild animals and birds. Photography and painting portraits of these has been a result of this. Most of my writing and poetry is of my experiences with a wide range of animals and birds. But my writing is in its infancy.

The sparrow hawk arrived in my garden two years ago.

The Sparrow Hawk

High summer garden full of song birds' trills
Sitting preening in the boughs of the yew
Large shadow falls, blots out the brilliant sun
The wing span of the sparrow hawk as it kills
Fear hangs in the air, blood mixes with dew
This scene creates sadness of a farmer's gun
Once happy garden is eerily silent
Where early alarm sounds swept from branch to branch
Survey months of carnage, sadness is pent
If I could go back and see that blood stanch
Beauty of this falcon is bitter-sweet
Plumage exquisite, its poise is elite
Blackbird, collar dove, wren, robin, all slain
Remnants all over the garden has lain.

Jenny Ambrose

Notes

I am 42 years old; married with two children. I live in Paisley and work as a molecular biologist in a busy haematology department in Glasgow.

Until now, apart from scientific papers, my only publications have been letters to newspapers.

My interests are: music (in particular church music), crafts and, recently, sketching and painting.

I wrote poetry as a teenager, mainly non-rhyming, and have only recently started writing again. Poetry is important to me - I frequently read it. This particular poem was written after I became a member of Paisley Abbey, in September 1996.

Belonging

At last it is completed
I really do belong
To this wonderful, old abbey;
Not just one among the throng
Of adherents and visitors
Who come only now and then
To sample the tranquillity
That's not of the world of men.

An autumn morn of sunshine,
Windows glowing in the light.
Voice and organ all combining
To make the whole scene right.
The warmth I felt surround me
On that St Mirin day
Makes me want to stay forever
To worship and to pray.

Then in the evening - compline,
That lovely, ancient rite.
Of men's voices chanting plainsong
For God's blessing on the night.
Can anyone who hears it
Not know it's from above?
And be moved to feel contentment
In the knowledge of God's love.

Fiona M Reid

Notes

John left a banking career to become a full time carer. He has a lifelong interest in poetry, but it was through meeting with a professional writer that he came to realise, more fully, the door that God was opening in his life. Since then, he has had over 700 poems published in various magazines and anthologies.

As a Christian poet with a sensitive approach, he is much in demand as a speaker at church fellowships.

John has a keen sense of humour: as well as several anthologies of Christian verse, he has had two short collections of humorous verse published.

From Here to Maternity!

She cried 'My baby's nearly due.
The pains are coming now!'
Her husband said, 'Don't panic dear.
I'll get you there somehow.'

He rushed her to the hospital,
but though he was quite swift
the baby didn't wait for him.
She had it in the lift!

She lay, embarrassed on the floor
and couldn't stop her tears.
The nurse was very kind to her
And said, 'There, there my dear.'

'At least the baby's fit and well
so don't get in a state.
One more won't make much difference.
This lift can carry eight!'

'We're used to strange things happening.
A mum a year ago
had her baby in the car park.
These things occur you know.'

She thought that this might cheer her up
but tears began anew,
and the mother said, 'I know.
That was my baby too!'

John Christopher

Bungee Jump

Notes

I would like to thank my wife, Ann, because if it wasn't for her prompting I would never have tried to get my work published. Also to my daughters Sian, Laura and Ella, from whom I get so many ideas for my poems.

I live in Worcester, where I work as a postman. This poem is about a friend of mine, Dave, who did a bungee jump for charity. He invited me to jump with him but I reluctantly (!) declined, thinking it would be safer to write than jump.

All my poems are about my family and friends. This is the first poem I have had published in a book, but some of my work has been used in several magazines and circulars.

Up and up our hero goes
To the top of the metal structure
I hope they tie the elastic tight
If it slips it will cause a rupture.

With elastic tied about his legs
He'll drop towards the ground
The only thought to cross his mind
Is to pray he's tightly bound.

To make a jump requires some nerve
It also takes some guts
We look on and admire his nerve
But hope we don't see his guts.

He'll take his time then make his jump
The crowd will stand aghast
If a mistake is made and he hits the ground
The jump will be his last.

People will remember this brave man
They will say he died with a smile
But how will they know it's the cheeks of his face
That they will see at the top of the pile.

Surely that's his face they'll say
His smile that was all full of fun
And suddenly they'll all realise
It's nose sticking out of his bum.

Ian Nunney

Notes

I am 20 years old and am currently enjoying a life of wild parties with my best friend, Allison, in Halifax, West Yorkshire. I grew up in a small farming village in Shropshire, called Tibberton, and began writing mainly to stem the boredom, although in such an old and rural village I was never short of inspiration.

I have written many poems and short stories but this is the first to be published, although I hope not the last.

The Battle Cry

Face to face, eye to eye
I hear the piercing battle cry
For on this cold dark lonely night
We must face each other and fight
The sounds of hooves, the glint of swords
The bloodthirsty gathering in their hordes
To fight as soldiers until death befalls
Within these grey stone castle walls
I fight for power, for honour and glory
You fight to prevent me telling your story
As princes we're born, as warriors we die
Once again I hear the battle cry
You clad in black, I clad in white
The tamed forces of good and evil fight
I live to protect, you live in sin
Onward, let the battle begin.

Jessika Carrera

Notes

I am 23 years old and live with my parents in London. I have been writing songs and poetry for a little over a year, as a hobby.

This is the first time I have submitted any work to be published.

At the time of writing this poem I was trying to justify my existence, and that of the human race, with the hope we are here with some greater purpose and meaning, rather than being here by chance alone.

This poem is dedicated to my grandmother who is no longer with us, except in my heart.

Home of the Banished

Were we all thrown down from heaven
Were we all angels in the beginning
Sent into this human form as a punishment
Sent to pay our penance
Is that how we came to be
One of heaven's outcasts
Angels that wouldn't conform
Angels that wanted to be free
And so we were shut out
Left in the cold, left to grow old
Eventually to disappear from this place
Left to roam in obscurity, to die in disgrace
Is this why the world was created
To be the home of the banished
Is that what this world is for.

Tony Robinson

Driftwood

Driftwood was once part of a galleon,
part of that ship in an era long gone
destroyed in war, smashed, left to the weather
sank to the bottom to rot forever.

Driftwood broke free, floated away
across oceans so wide and deep.
By continents and islands, will land one day,
what's done is done, no point to weep.

Lonely old, frightened cold,
drifts on, rides waves, deep sleep.
Time stands still, driftwood's long wait,
immortal peace, trapped by fate.

Wave battered, bleached by sun,
wind shattered, rotted by salt.
Struggles and fights still holds on,
slowly dying but not its fault.

Lonely old, frightened cold,
drifts on, rides waves, deep sleep.
Time stands still, driftwood's long wait,
immortal peace, trapped by fate.

Land ahead, waves bring forth,
sandy beach, rest at last.
Solid ground by the wet shore,
no more water, sanctuary.

Breakers approach, those massive waves,
tide comes in, launched onto stone.
Caught between rocks, driftwood is saved,
man walks by, picks it up, takes it home.

Befriended now, calm and safe,
no more drifting on, deep sleep.
Over now, no more long wait.
Question is answered now by fate.

Lies in a house, lovely and warm,
cosy, contented, innocent, smile.
Outside in the cold rages a storm,
driftwood relaxes, sleeps awhile.

Disturbed from sleep, taken from the floor,
picked up by the man, is lifted higher.
Driftwood awakes, is dreaming no more,
man lets go, throws driftwood onto the fire . . .

R Graeme Evans

The Mill

Notes

In 1944, the Allies bombed the dykes at Westkapelle, flooding Holland to drive out the occupying forces.

Standing on that dyke in April 1995, looking across the flat open land, I realised the Dutch people had no escape when the dykes broke and swept through their town, taking with it eight out of every ten houses, and that to live became a matter of luck.

I was told of 47 people who ran to the Mill for safety. The Mill survived but debris washed against the door and forty four people perished inside.

The Mill is a tribute to those people.

The dyke is breaking. 'Run!', they said. 'Run! Run! or we'll all be dead.'
They said, 'Run,' where shall we run? We did not know, nor anyone.

The dyke is breaking, 'Run and hide!' The dyke is breaking, 'Hide inside!'
Where shall we hide? Where shall we go? We did not know, we did not know.

There's no high ground, there is no hill. So forty ran towards the Mill.
Here's our high ground, here's where we'll hide. Then all the forty went
inside.

'Shut the door!' the people shout. 'That will keep the water out.'
'Shut the door, it's safe inside.' Inside the Mill is where we'll hide.

The waters pour across the land, smashing houses where they stand,
Tossing all up in the air. Except the Mill which stands four-square.

Through the dyke the waters pour. Then something jams the Mill house
door.
The people scream. The people shout. But no one's there to let them out.

The waters slowly fill the Mill, 'til all is silent, all is still.
Then, when the water leaves once more. There's forty dead behind the door.

Tony Fuller

184

I am Leaving . . .

Notes

Written in memory of a cherished friend - my mother. Without her encouragement and reassurance I wouldn't be where I am to-day.

A dedication to anyone suffering, or who has suffered, abuse. God bless you Mum.

Finally I have bought myself a ticket out,
I am leaving you today,
I can't take any more beatings,
I believe you should be locked away;
my bags are packed, I've left a note,
it will tell you why I have gone,
please don't try to find me,
it's too late now, what's done is done.
For years you have beaten me
and treated me like dirt,
I'm so tired of crying,
I'm afraid of the hurt.
You laughed each time you hit me,
you thought my pain was fun, but,
each time that you hit me,
the stronger I'd become.
My mind was made up the night
you hurt me with a knife,
from that moment on,
I was no longer your wife.
I'm leaving you now, I'm not coming back,
I can't go on waiting for every attack.
As I close the door behind me
I stop and question why . . .
I don't know of any reasons,
with burning tears I cry, all along
I loved you so much it hurts me to think
that you could cause me such pain,
so I am leaving you now,
I am not coming back, not ever, no never again . . .

Sharon Varley

Notes

Wun uv the Few

My name is Charlie Smith, I
write under the pen name of
Charlie Boy Smith. I am 72
years of age and I live in
the small market town of
Wymondham (pronounced
Windham), ten miles from
the city of Norwich, in Nor-
folk. I was born here, as was
my father and his father be-
fore him, and I am an ex-RAF
aircrew/teleprinter operator.

I've had thirty poems pub-
lished in various anthologies
and magazines, I also have an
album of songs, mostly in the
Norfolk dialect, and a single
disc, both A and B sides. I've a
book of my songs published
(music and words), and six-
teen songs I've written espe-
cially for a local folk singer
have been published on cas-
sette and CD. I have the abil-
ity to write a poem or song
within hours, sometimes only
minutes. I've written three
full length novels and forty or
so short stories (not published
yet).

My hobbies include playing
guitar, singing my songs and
doing crosswords but, as my
wife is poorly and needs 24
hour care, I am not able to
follow my own pursuits as I
would have liked.

I started writing poetry at the
age of nine, when both Mum
and Dad were in hospital, I
wrote weekly to Mum, in
verse, in the form of a poetic
diary (sadly, lost when they
moved house) which makes it
around thirty six years I've
been writing poems and
songs.

My inspiration comes from
anything and everything I
hear and see. *Wun uv the
Few* came about when visit-
ing hospital with Jean, my
wife; a local ex-pilot came in,
in a wheelchair, and the looks
he received from the sur-
rounding folk! (he was in the
way.) Well, that's all I
needed.

*I'd like to dedicate this poem
to Colin, (wun of the few).*

So slow did he walk, no payshense had I,
Cum on ow slow cooch I sed,
Yew musta bin born slow, yew silly ow man,
An he tanned an nodded his hed,
I yewsta be farst, meny yeer ago
Afore earj an pearn took thar toll,
But now I carn't travel as kwik as I'de like,
An this here stick I dew hatta hold,
But wen I wooz yung, I travelled reel farst,
In Spitfires an such did I fly,
An I searved the wald f'm Hitler's ow lot,
Tew keep yew alive did I try,
I lorst orl the yewss uv me arms an legs,
Up in the clowds and the blew,
Yiss bor, I wooz farst, much farster then,
Corse I wooz jiss wun uv the few.

Charlie Boy Smith

Always

You were always there,
And, I think that's what made it worse
Don't get me wrong
It wasn't bad
Just being there made it no good.
I thought about it.
I really did.
I thought what it would be like
For us to be *so* close,
But, we could never be *that*
Close,
Could we?
Always together,
But never close,
In our hearts we were always
Apart.
With our minds, we'll always
Be bound.
Always together
But never close.

Katie Marks

Nowhere to Hide

The sun is hot, its fierce heat reflecting off the walls,
Flower heads, feebly vying for its rays
There are no rainy days.
Grass no longer green, its roots you can almost hear them scream,
Screaming out for water that's been denied
     There's nowhere to hide

Bees buzzing round the weary flower heads, most of which are dead,
Soil turned to dust, like old bones left to rot,
The longest roots reaching for moisture deep below,
Even then they hardly grow.
Sunflowers! Heads turned to the sun, coarse and dried,
     There's nowhere to hide,

Relentless heat beating down on plants and trees, neither putting out their
                      seed,
Too weary, and tired, to make a show,
None, have the strength to grow,
There is no water, only heat and dust, but still into the air, the gas we thrust
All this colour we viewed is cast aside,
Because for them, like us
     There's nowhere to hide.

Blanche Middleton

Notes

I am aged 49 years young! I have two sons and one beautiful granddaughter. I work from home, organising events for shopping centres. We live in Tenby, Wales, in sight of the sea.

Hobbies and interests? Jack of all trades and master of none.

I started writing poetry whilst living in isolation on a smallholding, with two young sons to care for. I have been writing for over twenty years and it is mainly my emotions that inspire me to write. Writing down my thoughts has helped me through the peaks and troughs of life.

The poem is dedicated to the love of my heart - Robbo - we married in Tuscany in October 1996, with the blessing of his and my children.

For the Love of My Heart

I looked but could not see,
I heard but did not listen,
A soul locked within its prison.

No one understood,
Or if they ever could,
I would not share it,
For fear it would break.

There was always someone in the shadows,
Urging me on,
Making me learn what I felt,
Was not wrong.

The shadows became a form
That engulfed my soul,
And there you were before me,
My warrior of old.

Only seconds of misunderstanding,
Years of love and sharing,
I listened, I heard, I saw,
And love the person you are to me, sweet and caring.

Steps still un-taken,
Words left unsaid,
Today is our future,
Tomorrow is in my head.

Betty Ann Collins

Notes

George Aubrey Henstock was born in 1924, in Newark, Nottinghamshire, the eldest of nine children. He is divorced and has two children, Paul and Avril.

He has a City and Guilds First Class for bread and floor confectionery and is a retired BT district catering manager, with fifty years catering experience.

His hobbies include wine making, food and wine, gardening, travel and motoring to catering exhibitions.

The poem, *The Sands of Time*, was published by The Society of Poets in their anthology, *The Other Side of the Mirror*. He was awarded a certificate of merit.

Writing poetry began as a fun thing between work colleagues, writing about each other, about twelve years ago.

Inspiration comes from mood swings, situations, or romantic events - often when depressed, when he puts his thoughts and feelings in writing, to release them. As a child, his mother was always quoting snippets of poetry - perhaps she was unable to fulfil her dreams, having to bring up a large family. Sometimes, Aubrey feels that he is writing for her.

'There is no greater love than that of a mother for her child and those words of wisdom she speaks in its memory filed.'

The inspiration for this particular poem came whilst talking to people. Quite often they would say 'Ah well, that's part of life's tapestry.'

It is dedicated to a very special friend.

The Tapestry of Life

Our tapestry of life began the day we were conceived
Each stitch carefully placed whilst suckling on our mother's knee
We could never know what the final picture would be
A new needle a different thread, we learn to walk with a wobbly tread
We tried to stand, always held by those skilful hands
Another stitch, another strand and now to talk to learn and understand
That first square is now complete we've learned to talk and stand on our
own two feet.

The second phase has now begun, no longer do we dribble and drool
Those threads of knowledge are gained at school
Successes and failures carefully traced each stitch carefully tied
And carefully placed, with sadness and joy but never misplaced
Those stitches of time go slowly on, with different threads and a different
hue.

A change takes place, a change in you, in life we learn to read
And write of geography, history and all its might
Also we've learned what's right and wrong
But the tapestry of life keeps going on and on
We strive to compete to achieve and shout with pride of all that we have
won.

We share with friends those halcyon days of carefree fun
But all too soon time to leave another square has begun
This the largest square of all, it will show our achievements successes and
failures in all that we do
And like the seasons with the sun and the rain
It will show the hardships, anguish and pain, perhaps of a love in vain
The threads will be taut and tense some will eventually break
But the tapestry must go on, those threads are tied, we start again some to
failure some to fame.
But slowly and surely those stitches completing the tapestry frame
All pulled together for those careful and gentle hands to mend
And continuing to our tapestry end
A complete picture of life's evolution parts of which there is
No easy solution, and sadly a tapestry no one will ever see
Bright with love and fond affection of a friend that is so dear to me
And one full of beautiful memories that is my life's tapestry.

Aubrey Henstock

Rain

Notes

I am a great-grandmother living in the old market town of Hailsham, in East Sussex. I have always written, mostly children's books and poetry. I have been fortunate to have had a children's book published, called Stories and Verses for the Very Young, when my children were very young. They were my inspiration.

I have won the Civil Service Literary Award for poetry and have had a lot of other pieces of poetry, as well as prefaces, published.

My children and the beautiful countryside are all the inspiration I need. My writing is my hobby. Living the life of raincoats and wellingtons in the country, my poem *Rain* seemed so right.

Feeling the rain so fierce and strong,
      Driven by wind with its soaring song,
            Furious splashing, angry splashing,
                  Everyone running, darting, dashing,
                        Into the dry, laughing, panting,
                              Glad to get out of the watery ranting.

Listening to its crisp pit pat,
      The dog stirs restlessly on the mat,
            The fire draws well, sends showers of sparks,
                  Through the chimney to meet the dark,
                        But nobody cares we're safe and snug,
                              With warming drinks from brimming
                                          mugs

The early morning dawn's so still,
      The sun creeps gently over the sill
            Quietly dripping earth so clean,
                  No one would know of the torment there'd been,
                        But slowly everything comes to life,
                              Forgotten already the hours of strife,

Till the rain and the wind comes again one night.

Peggy A Oliver

Bed of Roses

For Mary, my only love.

I am to you, a tender warm breeze
a silent ocean current
graceful with ease.
I dream of you, night and day
and forever and ever
so please don't drift away.
My love for you fills this shallow heart
so kiss and hug me now
before it falls apart.
A bed of roses
and the lights are low
the curtains are down
the candles aglow.
I whisper these words when we're together
my deep affection forever and ever.

Stephen Roberts

A Writer's Lament

Notes

A retired psychiatric nurse, I am married with a 20 year old son. My sisters and mother also write, and my sister-in-law is a published novelist. I am an ex-Trade Union Branch Secretary, and have held office in numerous clubs.

My hobbies include photography, magic, playing the organ, reading (especially psychology, history and science), and writing.

An old word processor has increased and improved my output. My verses are inspired by reflections on the value of the pen, typewriter and word processor, and quality versus quantity.

Dedicated to all who ever encouraged me, whether they knew it or not.

Note: Mal de mer - sea sickness.

How could Dickens write at all
    When so depressed and ill?
How could Shakespeare write so much
    With nothing but a quill?

How could Milton write his stuff?
    He couldn't even see.
How could Alexander rule the world
    At half the age of me?

How could Beethoven write music
    That he could never hear?
How could Nelson be so great
    And still have mal de mer?

I'm not depressed or blind or deaf,
    Or made ill by the sea.
I've no handicaps or things like that;
    Life's full of help for me.

Of these great lives I've been well taught.
    Their stories and their battles fought,
I've read their books, I've heard their play:
    So . . . why can I not do as they?

Robert Leonard Cooper

Notes

I am 34 years of age and I have lived most of my life in South London. I am presently working as a motor cycle courier. I am also studying Homeopathy which I hope to pursue as a career, once I have qualified.

With reference to this poem; I must point out the obvious fact that I am a keen cyclist and motor cyclist, and have been for many years. I was fortunate to discover, through forces beyond my control, the parallels between one's existence and poetry. Symmetry, continuity, balance, mystique, sensation, imagination, pain, joy, sound, insight, spirituality and love. These things, plus many other factors, don't just apply to life and poetry, but also to being on two wheels.

Two Wheels

How it feels
To be on two wheels
The wondrous feeling
With which you are dealing
But not always straight
Though I do really rate
The desirable need for angle and speed
But not always so
'Cos I like to go slow.

Francis Xavier Patron

My name is Rebecca Naomi Hazell. I am aged 9 years. My interests are lizards, sharks and I love animals. My hobbies are rugby, netball, football and swimming.

I have two brothers called Luke (7) and Joel (5).

My mum and dad's names are Lynn and Dominic.

I have a dog called Max and two lizards called Lizz and Titch. We have rabbits, guinea pigs, birds and fish.

By Grandma:

Rebecca has been writing poems all this year, which seem to be first impressions. Menorca was written soon after her arrival there - her first visit abroad.

Menorca

Menorca is a pretty place, swimming pools,
the nice hot sun, places to go, places to see.
The hot smell of Spanish food
and all the pretty houses and the smell of
the salty sea and the sandy beach.

Rebecca Hazell (8)

Notes

I'm 18 years old. I work in a restaurant at a Sainsbury superstore in Frome, Somerset, and have my own flat nearby. I enjoy nightclubbing and socialising at weekends.

I have been writing poems since I was 14. Two of my poems have been published in anthologies.

Seeing how much violence is increasing in our world gave me the inspiration to write this poem. It is a youngster's view of living in a nation where peace seems impossible and holding onto your dreams is the only way to survive. I believe everyone can bring their dreams into reality.

War in Our World

Everyday we all awake with the fear of there being no tomorrow
each day is a threat
wanting to forget
living with this fear and this sorrow.
How much more fighting
how much more killings
how many lives are at stake, are at cost
on with this bitterness
this horror
this hatred
aiming nowhere
gaining nothing but lives lost.
For us we are young and want to live our lives
we have so much to give for our future
how can we live with so many scars hid inside
why should we grow up in this fear living torture.
Hope is all we need it's hope that keeps us going
what else do we have except for hope
how do we know that we won't die tomorrow
how do they expect us to cope.
I would like our world to be a free smiling nation
walk down a street and feel safe round every bend
I know sometime in the future
this war will be over
I just hope I am here to see it end.

Karen Baker

Notes

I am a Scot by birth and have always lived here. I am 48 years old, married to Jim for twenty seven years and we have two grown-up children, Neil and Kirsty. I live in a rural village, Saline in Fife.

I have been writing poetry for over twenty five years. This is the first time in print!

My elderly friends inspired me to write this particular poem. They taught me about life and what it means to have Jesus Christ in my heart, so this poem is dedicated to them all, past and present.

World in a Room

For years she sat in the same spot,
The same chair,
The ordinary room.
Old grey photographs on the dressing table
Loved ones she can't even remember
They don't come to see her.
Cold tea in a cup with a ring round the top,
Half a digestive, and crumbs.

The carer comes in and smiles,
No speaking,
Takes the cup and goes
Other people to see, more to do.
A bird outside at the peanuts
Holds her interest for a moment,
Places to go, things to do
Birds don't stay long.

Will someone come tonight?
Someone that knows and loves her
Will she know them?
Will they talk politely for a while?
Then go away
Will she care?

The carer, more tea and a biscuit
Turns down the covers,
Gets her ready for bed.
No radio tonight?
The old grey photographs will do.
'Goodnight' comes a little voice,
Did she hear me? Does she care?

Janette H McNaught

Sandra, at times, is two bob short of a quid and says the dumbest things. This happened one day - I lost the grip of my perch and told her she was a bloody half-wit! This set us to calculating the sum between wit, witless and half-wit. On trying to relay the topic of our mirth to my wallet (the hubby), as usual, something in the air between my mouth and Terry's ears made this impossible, so 'the ode' was born, only to be read by myself and my sneaky sister, who sent it to Poetry Today. Thanks, Moya!

Think About It

A wit with dryish humour,
I hear are very few.
Considered to be very sharp,
That leaves out me and you.

A no wit, hasn't laughter,
Not even in his dreams.
Still, not thought of as a dullard,
Just lives his life, it seems.

That leaves a large proportion
Of people, you will find;
That must be classed as *half wits*,
Why is that? So unkind!

A no wit on the bottom,
The wit, is on the top.
While we, *found in the middle*,
It's us that cops the lot!

My maths there is no changing,
You can't mutate the sum,
That half is always better;
Than ever having none.

Joan McCormick

Untitled

Drifting in and out,
I walk along its very edge,
And hear its promises, gently beckon me.
Its darkness is complete,
Only patterns of thought trace across my mind.
This fight I long to lose.
And slowly I slip into her warm embrace,
Longing to be as one.
Who knows where we will travel,
Or how the scattered images of unconsciousness
Will fill those dark hours.
Further and deeper I fall.
Until only my eyelids flicker,
Like the faint pulse of a dying man.
All the world I know, and a world I don't,
Surge thru my motionless body,
Tears and sweat stain linen white,
And a silent voice screams,
At the demons in my head.
Then at last, oxygen pumps round muscles tight,
As I stretch to welcome the dawn,
Of a new day.

Paul Hope

Sorrow is a Misery so Hollow

I've never quite said,
what I've wanted to say.
Even though I've tried,
I can't forget my yesterdays.
Words are a good way,
of explaining the way I feel.
But love is unexplainable,
and love is what I feel.
I've walked down a long path,
and darkness has followed.
A pain is still present, and,
my heart is full of sorrow.
I have said the goodbyes
I never wanted to say.
I know I made a mistake,
the path, led the wrong way.
Would I meet you here tomorrow,
if I asked you not to follow?
My heart is full of sadness,
- a misery - so hollow.
The hollowness of which I know,
can never be denied.
Sadness is what I feel,
it's the darkest place inside.

Shane Welch

Notes

I was born in 1975. and am the eldest of 4 children, to parents who are an inspiration. I am involved in horse breeding and training and Newcastle West in County Limerick is my home town. I lived in Bristol and now live in Holland. Travel is the spice of life 'I think'. This is my first published poem but I started writing poetry at 14 years old. Much of my work was lost in a fire.

Harlequin

Suddenly the brave knight slays the harlequin . . .

Hush, complete silence,
Lights are brought down.
Children fall back in their seats
Wide screaming mouths, nest of feeding birds
Closed shut now.
One child crushed a crisp in its mouth
The sound was deafening.
Closed faces in a picture of disbelief
A lifeless Muse, atmosphere died.
Died with the harlequin, the tragic hero met his fate
Lying there on stage, lifeless
Looking a lot smaller now
Warm tears trickled down the cheeks of some witnesses
To this terrible occasion

Blast, lights thrown on red, blue, yellow
On and off like a throbbing thumb
The buffoon, the jester bounds twenty feet into the air
Whilst executing a triple somersault
A headstand followed
Now the circus melody blasted out.
There he stood twenty feet tall
Donned in a red mask, palm tree-like hat, blue and black
Supporting bells on each leaf
Green slippers and bright jingling bells, red tights
What a magnificent sight
Children leap in spontaneous frenzy
Spring-loaded chairs shoot back
Refreshments thrown in the air
Mineral bottles knocked and kicked over
The lion had killed the Jew in the ancient amphitheatre
The Romans cried for more: hooray!

The harlequin lives on for another scene.

Jonathan William Dunne

Serpentine Siesta . . .

The lacy leaves of early spring, on a hillside's verdant slopes,
A gnarled and twisted elder, with its sheltering branches droop't
By mossy, primros'd clumps, where in crafty ambush, lies
A snake, with softly darting tongue, and agate eyes.

Flat head swaying, a gently soughing hiss.
Mesmerising movements, for its target, just one
Small rabbit, too terrified for flight.
One second more of stillness, then a blur of prism'd light.

A writhing sinuosity of iridescent scales,
Folding plumply, coil on coil, merged with earthy clay.
Hinged jaws, agape, with convulsive, gulping speed,
Devouring, headfirst, its wildly kicking, agitated prey.

Thus settling, in bulging, satisfied repletion,
To serpentine siesta, digestive moratorium.

Marjorie Chapman

Stained Glass Dream

Now aged 27, I began writing
poetry a little over a year ago,
and this is the first time I
have offered my work for
wider consideration in any
way.

I find that poetry provides a
fulfilling way of expressing
the creative element of my
nature. Often, it is only after
writing about something that
I become aware of what I
really think and feel about it.

Particularly effective turns of
phrase, including some here,
can spring to mind at almost
any time and I find it helps
greatly to write these down
quickly, in case they are for-
gotten.

Enclosed within my prescribed dimensions I understood
how light shines most brightly where once all was empty and dull.
For gleaming rays and beams brought you shimmering before me,
pouring richness of colour into a life of cold and grey.
You held a magical crescent,
in my vision fluorescent,
as you became my stained glass dream.

Suspended in crystal air, so pure, gentle and clean,
how was I to know that it was not for me that you shone?
A mirror in time had reflected you here by chance,
yet I found my reflection merged with yours in the window.
I could not help myself feeling,
that I wished I was kneeling,
at your feet in my stained glass dream.

Opening myself toward you I searched deeper within me,
finding presents to give you that I never knew I had.
Tenderly I kindled my votive candle, in whose glow
your special rainbow sparkle danced brightly and drew me on.
Happily I glided through space,
preparing to take my place,
beside you in my stained glass dream.

Yet as I moved on you retreated twice as far again,
the air cooled and a chill unease descended upon me.
Your face looked paler as the light fought to pass the frosting glaze,
your eyes grew opaque, the foretelling of my fall transparent.
I knew that a new day once-born,
given with only one dawn,
was dying in my stained glass dream.

The dream's ending sliced across the heavily sighing air,
catching me in a shower of spinning spear-pointed shards.
Disconnected fragments, each with part of my reflection,
cascaded to the ground, carrying me down in their embrace.
I fell shocked and shaken and blind,
leaving my senses behind,
smashed along with my stained glass dream.

Neil A Rundle

Notes

Stan Hodson is presently (until mid-May 1997) Lord Mayor of Coventry. He was born on 5th October 1929, is a retired financial consultant and lives (and was born) in Coventry.

Stan has written and had published hundreds of articles to newspapers, financial journals and magazines, and recently wrote a foreword to Images of the Past, concerned with medieval, pre-war and post-war Coventry, recently published.

Stan has only ever written for the satisfaction of having views expressed, in an attempt to influence opinion and, in financial journals, to participate in marketing and conservation ideas. No monetary prizes have ever been sought or awarded.

Stan has an overwhelming urge to express condolences at a time when, it seems, civilisation has become hopeless. As first citizen elect, it seemed a compelling quest and Stan has never written poetry previously. Stan believes that it is the written word that is most compelling.

The pen is mightier than the sword!

Song of Dunblane

Why were these lambs subjected to this slaughter,
Could easily have been our own son or daughter.
Defenceless and helpless save for courageous teacher devotion
Who, just then, had thought that sheep may safely graze, then made
                                                    that motion
To protect these innocents, so little and young, but old enough for
                                                    saintliness,
In this season of rebirth, these brave little mites will inherit the earth while
                        trudging a tragic, indelible route to Godliness.

A disturbed mind, craving to be understood, took refuge in cowardice and
                                    evil, with faith in guns,
A school doth not a prison make, it is not the school that is unsafe, but the
                        unsuspected derangement of unsuspected sons
Breathtaking, stupefying in its proportions, these children and their beloved
                                    teacher are immortalised,
We lend them our tears and salute them with silence,
We pray for their parents, for an end to gun violence.

What have we learned from this unspeakable act?
Are we to sacrifice young blood in the name of personal rights and
                                                    freedom?
Can we, with certainty remove the hazard from life with locks and bars,
Or should we show them down the paths of peace with God to lead them
We shall remember them as if they were our own,
God's immortal children, now safe in the arms of their maker.
We will only remember them as the loving children they were in that town,
With only the heavenly Father as heaven's awakener.

Stan Hodson

Basking in Loneliness

Vivid recollection of a landscape once green
Myriad emotion setting the scene
Cool summer morns laid by her side
Pilgrimage to satisfy hope and pride
Fulfilment of lifetime ambition, a goal
To bury part of me in the root of her soul
And now I've completed the principle task
Within these rays of loneliness my body may bask
For although we're not together, how can we be apart?
Distance fails to diminish the power of my heart.

Leigh J Hadaway

Notes

I was born on 24 January 1964 in Guildford, Surrey, my parents are Frank and Audrey Clark and I have been writing poetry for ten years.

I have had some of my work published by various poetry publishers and I am presently involved in two poetry competitions.

I enjoy writing romantic rhyming poetry. My poetry has been inspired by my former girlfriend, Mary. I believe that poetry is for everyone and that there is a place for it in the modern world.

Stung

She stung deep inside of me -
That I clung to her sea.
My feelings burned -
As I gradually learned
Of a love so rewarding
I welcomed her sting.

This girl I had sought -
So willingly caught
Me in her clasp -
As I had to grasp
Her compelling gaze
Which transformed into a heavenly haze.

I lovingly adored
The girl whose love I stored.
I became bewitchingly captivated
In an affection which was fated.

She made my senses tingle so -
I was captivated by her beauty,
Never wanting to let go,
As her power raged strongly.

Stephen Clark

A Child is a Child and a Woman is a Woman?

Notes

I am 21 years old and this is the first piece of my writing I have had published.

I would like to dedicate this achievement to my Grandpa.

This poem is not meant to be aggressive, but to make people stop and think, in order to find the compassion which I believe everyone is capable of.

The scream echoed around the world;
The cry was taken up by millions;
To the east and west,
To the north and south - all, every, each

She was alone, struggling for space.
She was alive, surrounded by the dead, still competing for air.
She was starving, she was freezing, she was naked.

The world spat on her.
The world kicked her.
The world despised her.

Does the glass shake in your hand?

Mary Dawson

Notes

I am Irish, now living in England and have been working for the past two years as a cabin crew member with British Airways short-haul at Gatwick, which I love as I am surrounded by interesting, different people everyday.

Before I left Ireland, I studied for five years at two different universities, attaining a BA in Sociology and German. I then went on to do a Post-graduate degree in Journalism and Media Studies, where my love for words grew. I have been working on my own Irish novel for many years. I have written many short articles for a main Irish newspaper concerning social and political issues; writing gives me a certain indescribable freedom.

Poor Little Girl

She sat alone on a bridge
her face red and sore
through her weak bones
the chill wind did bore
amidst a Christmas rush
the people dash by
her tears go unnoticed
her pain, her cry

'Pay no attention, it's a stunt' they say
but that won't make the problem go away
at Christmas we should help and give
a chance for hope, a chance to let live

What can be done
to erase such pains
to stop the pursuit of selfish aims
hold out a hand to touch her face
give chase to the harsh coldness
of this place.

Sinéad Comerford

Animus Paucorum
(The Spirit of the Few)

What happened to the spirit of the men who flew the skies?
The men to whom so many said their sad but proud goodbyes;
Does that spirit flourish in the people of today -
Or has it too like many things, gone old and passed away?

They came from many places - from the cities, from the towns;
From the villages and farms, from the valleys, hills and downs;
They died in many places, some far from home apart;
Did those who prayed and waited hear an echo from their heart?

Hear the sound of aircraft rising o'er the swell of clouds on high;
The enemy approaching fast, the battle in the sky;
The loops, the dives, the dogfights happening high above the earth;
The black plume and the spiral taking someone on to death.

A man who spoke for Britain said in words so very true -
That never was so much due from so many to so few;
And if time's passage took us on a thousand years or more -
That we should still remember them, and Britain's finest hour.

The man who spoke for Britain lies at rest in Bladon's Field;
Was he the last of the bulldog breed - to fight and never yield?
And does his spirit flourish in the people of today,
Or has it too like many things, gone old and passed away?

When night-time's silent watches let memory hold the door;
In the mind's eye there are images of faces seen no more;
We know, whether morning brings dark clouds or sunshine's ray -
That for all of our tomorrows, they gave their today.

They lie at rest 'neath serried ranks of simple sacred stone;
In foreign field's far corners, forever Britain's own;
They lie in many places, their sacrifice all done;
Inheritors of the valiant years, we hold the heights they won.

The grand old tunes of glory still stir the pulsing blood;
They help us to remember those who were taken at life's flood;
For them, what they fought and died for, we assert with renewed will,
That the spirit of our nation is alive and thriving still.

Simon Carrley

Notes

Now living in South Yorkshire, Simon spent nine years in the RAF and then became a civil servant. Since retirement, he is free to give more time to reading, including the works of many poets. He particularly likes the poetry of Thomas Grey, Emily Dickinson, Walter de la Mere and James Elroy Flecker.

This poem was inspired by his admiration for those who played such a pivotal role at a crucial time in British history.

The poem is dedicated to his wife and family.

From our house we look across a field straight up to the downs. Every day we watch the pattern of the shadows changing as the sun moves across the sky. In spring and autumn we can see the changing colours of the leaves in the wooded hanger opposite us. Figures of walkers are silhouetted against the skyline as they progress along the South Downs' Way.

I wrote this little poem for my granddaughter, Caroline. She will be surprised to see it in print. I hope she will like it.

Spring

Beneath the downs
They hid the clowns
And brought them out
On clowning day.
When I went up
They'd let them out
Falling about
Upping and downing
Dancing and clowning!
O clowns ahoy!
What joy, what joy!

John A Cole

Angling

Hook line sinker and float
Done from the bank or done from a boat
Disgorge the hook from fish's throat
Weight and measure jot down a note
If a tiddler kept in a jar
Bound to elaborate when stood at the bar
Sea or coarse fishing drycast or fly
Without lots of patience anglers would die
Maggots or gentles or just a worm
Makes the timorous shiver and squirm
Whether a holiday or just a weekend
Can make a day out for family and friends
If be a loner or angling club
Makes up a topic when retired to the pub.

Francis Arthur Rawlinson

An Alien Encounter

Hello! Little man
From way out in the blue.
Are you thinking of me
What I'm thinking of you?

Has this craft that you've come in
With strange light and sound
An intent to harm me
For reason unfound?

I offer my hand
And my heart's for the taking,
If you're coming in peace
I'm a friend in the making.

I'm eager to listen -
I've so much to learn
And your daunting appearance
Is not my concern.

We are floundering here
On this planet of ours,
And would welcome advice,
Be it coming from Mars!

I'll come with you gladly
On a journey through time
If you'll tell me the secret
To halt our decline.

There are others who'll join me
In search of this prize,
Who know that our future
Lies up in the skies.

So I'm begging you please
Do not turn me away,
As I'd welcome your blessing
And a permit to stay.

Phillippa M Benson

Notes

I was born in Halstead, Essex and educated at the Grammar School. I loved literature at an early age and always held a pen. Now in my middle sixties and recently widowed, I live in a village and adore nature.

My hobbies were embroidery, painting, gardening and decorating; curtailed now because of arthritis.

The spoken and written word is precious, so I made a commonplace book, for my poetry and favourite poems from other poets. It's very special.

Success began with a Valentine to my husband, in a Radio 2 competition in 1983, read on the air by Ian Ogilvy. Competitions entered before then had been rewarded by book tokens.

I gained joint second prize of £50 in 1995, when successful in a competition by the Poetry Institute of the British Isles. I now have poetry published in twelve books. My aim is to keep writing and to improve my style.

The Haven

When whistling winter winds wail round the cottage small,
And shake each shrub and hedge, and bend the trees so tall.
Then safe within the walls so thick and stout
With glowing fires so bright, to keep cold winter out,
A treasure house of store is found therein,
Till warmth and growth returns, to welcome spring.

When blinding snow storms swirl around from hills so high,
And daylight hours are darkened by the gloomy sky,
Then hyacinths, when planted in the fall
Glow like precious jewels. Their perfume fills the hall.
A sign of hope, till warmer days are seen.
When all the earth is clad in gentle green.

The ash logs stacked in rows against the wall, provide
The very best of warmth, and in the fire-side wide
Burn bright, and apple wood with fragrance sweet
Perfumes the air around, yet gives a gentle heat.
And work done during summer now ensures
Blest comforts, ere the winter time endures.

A dark dry downstair den reveals its secret hoard.
Where row on row, the bottled fruits and jams are stored.
Whilst pickles and preserves of every kind
Are labelled clearly, so much easier to find
With pots of honey made by busy bees,
And cooking apples from the orchard's trees.

The bounties of the fertile soil packed in the shed
'Neath paper, sacks, and straw, to make a cosy bed.
The gleaming implements of toil are neatly stacked,
And eating apples gleam from where they're racked.
The jacket, boots, and straw hat, safe from rain.
Till next year's planting time comes round again.

Come chilly nights of frost, come winter winds that blow.
Come howling gales that whirl the dancing flakes of snow.
Within this haven of content and rest
With books for company, beside a fire-side blest,
May peace abide, and music fill the hours,
Till blackbirds call, and earth sends forth her flowers.

Angela Douse

Notes

Chris Mosey earns his living as a freelance journalist and photographer. He was formerly correspondent in Scandinavia for The Times and The Observer.

He is the author of Cruel Awakening, Sweden and the Killing of Olof Palme (Hurst, London and St Martin's, New York) and the Fodor's Sweden guide book. He recently completed his first novel, The Nostradamus Connection, and wrote this poem in a small village in the hills of Provence, while working on that. He also plays guitar and writes songs.

Prayer

There is gold
In the morning

In the light
On the hills

In the calm
That calls you back

To who you are
And what you're doing here

This is for when you next forget:

Behind the hills,
Behind your flesh,
Behind the sky

Behind the lie
The blind men made

Raw energy glows
Cruel and bright as love

The centre of the earth is on fire
Your heart wears no price tag

Your friend the west wind blows free
Your breath is unlabelled

And out of the abyss
Your own voice whispers:
'This
And only this

Is worth your praise'

Chris Mosey

Notes

The Abyss serves as a metaphor for my sense of loss in this world, a world so full of meaning and mystery that not everything about it could be possibly understood in a lifetime. This feeling of loss stems from my knowledge that not everything can be explained such as who we really are as people, why we are really here and how life began; thus my true roots will always be 'black' (within the dust), my vision of the world 'lost' (curious to see the unknown) and my ultimate desire is to have these thoughts come to an end.

The Abyss

My eyes
Deceive me
Do they?
Reality
I think
This is,
I am who I am
Am I?
This mirror
Presents
Nothing different
Only
What we know
Mist
I now see
Lost
Shall I
Ever
Be found?

Among the clouds
I live,
Waiting
For
My feet to
Touch
The ground.

My roots -
Black
My vision?
I have no vision
These days provide
No explanation
These thoughts
Have no end

Natalie Robinson

Cardboard City

Notes

I am an administration officer for the local authority, aged 48 years, mother of Mark and Lisa and married for 27 happy years to Harvey, a project manager for a lighting company.

I have only recently begun to write poetry and have not attempted to have anything published previously. I am motivated to write mostly by a strong social conscience, injustice and inhumanity.

This poem was inspired following a trip to London, seeing the plight of the homeless and hungry.

Walls of boxes, newspaper sheets,
Nothing much covers the soles of his feet,
Splash, pitter-pat calls rain-soaked streets,
Dawn comes to cardboard city.

Stiffened old bones, coldly aching,
Prod fitful slumbers into awakening,
Gnawing hunger brings on the shaking,
That's life in cardboard city!

Scavenged dog-ends, roll another smoke,
A swig from a bottle making him choke,
Begging coppers from better-off folk,
What a life in cardboard city!

'No job, no home - help if you can -
I'm a vet, you know, from Vietnam,
Don't pass by me, good Samaritan,'
Life's hell in cardboard city!

Business over, a train to catch,
A hot meal to eat and TV to watch.
Will you give a thought to the filthy wretch
Who lives in cardboard city?

Hot soup and toast and mended shoes,
Conscience money - they paid their dues.
Got a bigger box, fresh sheets of news -
Life's good in cardboard city!

Kath Wiles

The Aged Inmates

These are our brothers,
               yours and mine,
Like ships that are wrecked
               on the rocks of time.
The flotsam of life's
               storm-tossed tide,
Broken and battered,
               and cast aside.
'Til on some strange
               secluded shore,
Their voyage is over
               for ever more.
Left high and dry
               by life's receding tide,
'Til the Beachcomber,
               arms open wide,
Gathers them lovingly
               to His side.

Christine May

Time Warp

Notes

I have now reached pensioner's age so-called, but I do not feel old; I live in Lichfield in Staffordshire, although I was born many miles away in Northumberland, a place called Newbiggin-by-the-Sea.

I have had a few poems published in various anthologies, including one about Dr Samuel Johnson, and one called *Minnie's Christmas*, about my Yorkshire terrier. Memories are special to me and these, along with unusual circumstances over the years, are inspirational.

My main hobby is writing poetry and short stories. I like walking very much, and also swimming. I suppose I began writing verse as a child living in Northumberland.

In my poem, *Time Warp*, I am visiting my childhood friends and once again recapturing the special happy years. People were not very well-off financially.

Where are all the children
I played with as a child?
Are they in some *time warp* cast
Clinging to that precious past?

If only I could enter in
And play those games again
The whip, with top, chalked-on design
Spinning, spinning, on and on
The skipping-rope, and happy chanting song
'Come on, jump in and out' happy hours long

We used to have a home-made tent
With clothes-horse against the railings
And a sheet, would be the roof and walls
'But oh the blissful hours spent'
The games played out, in this special tent

'Come on Margaret, have a cup of tea!'
'Where is Gloria, home is she?'
'It's hot today, so find some shade'
'Come have some home-made lemonade'

'Look there is my brother David
On his roller-skates'
Leaning, somewhat shakily by the garden gate
Now I can see Alan, playing hide and seek
And is that Mary, having a little weep?

Now the light is changing the street lights have come on
But still the children play their games
'Edith your mother calls.' 'It's supper time'
Must I leave this place, no please
Just ten minutes more!
Soon the darkness is all around
And tired children and sleepy town
Another day some other place
In which to play, play, play!

I shall keep my *time-warp*
And enter when I will
No one can take the memories
For they shall linger still
And I shall visit often
To see my childhood friends
I know they wish to see me
For they are in time without an end!

Mavis Dickinson

Notes

I was born in 1962; my parents are Brian and Catherine Rowan. I am married to Teresa and we have two children: Mark who is 5 years old and Amy, just 5 months. I went to St Kevin's Comprehensive in Kirkby and then Teesside Polytechnic in Middlesbrough, gaining a BA in Business Studies. I now work as a marketing assistant.

I have two poems published: *A Lost Soul* in The Other Side of the Mirror (October 1996), and *A Father's Son* in Awaken to a Dream (January 1997) both published by The International Society of Poets.

In February 1996, I entered a competition, resulting in *A Lost Soul* being published. Previously my work has been hidden away in a box. I have been writing since 1980.

I am inspired by my own conflict of thought, and as such, my writing is often an emotional release. I hope it provokes thought and provides pleasure.

Grief describes my experience of funerals. Initial sadness through to stories of the deceased. Often these are humorous and almost suggest a part of the person lives on in others.

Grief

Sorrow turns to grief,
When to all around is seen a wreath,
For relatives and friends untold,
And life has passed and stories told,
Of joy and happiness that passed,
And for each one it is a task.

And so for each mourner called,
A memory of life that changed,
The memories of those remained,
And in unison the congregation rise,
To savour all that they had known,
Of the life that had grown,
Within a feeling of their own.

Kevin Rowan

New World

One vision, one dream, a future of peace.
Time for the suffering and killing to cease,
It's in our hands, our destiny and fate,
To take control of our lives, before it's too late.
So much to give, but always we take,
Never we realise how much is at stake.
Open your eyes, your mind and your heart,
Create a new world, and make a fresh start.
The same old mistakes, day after day,
We don't see the effects, and the high price we pay,
Blinded by ignorance, overcome with our fears,
The pleas and the cries, only fall on deaf ears.
Our planet is screaming with frustration and pain,
But we still rape the land, again and again,
Hear my message, my desperate cry,
Change what is happening, or we surely must die.

Michelle Jeffrey

The Invading Christ

Notes

I am a retired Baptist minister, living in the West Midlands. Most of the poems I have written were used in Christmas or Easter cards, distributed by the church of which I was then pastor.

Triumph House of Peterborough have published several of these poems. In addition, several articles and sermons have appeared in the local press, the Baptist Times, the Christian Herald and Expository Times.

For the past few years, I have also been engaged in writing stories for our grandchildren.

They sealed the guarded tomb,
Confident, now His voice was stilled,
That they had banished every trace
Belonging to the man just killed;
But angels rolled the stone away,
Revealed He was no longer there,
Raised by the power of God to live
And show His presence everywhere.

They barred the wooden door,
Afraid that foes might find them there,
For who could face if they were caught
The fate that they might have to bear?
But Christ passed through the gate of fear,
To calm their souls and give them peace,
To nerve their arm for future fight,
And give their troubled souls release.

They closed their darkened minds,
Ignoring what the Scriptures said,
Thinking their faith in Him misplaced,
And feeling that their hope was dead;
But Christ came to them on the road,
To lift the cloud and light a flame,
Which sent them back with new-found zeal,
To preach to all His peerless name.

There is no way to keep Him out,
Power must yield and fear depart,
Gloom cannot linger when He comes
To cheer the faint and broken heart;
Jesus can meet us where He will,
Eat at our meals and walk our way,
Nothing can stop the Lord of life,
Who leads us into endless day.

Fred Stainthorpe

Lone Star

I live in a beautiful Wiltshire village. This will be the third poem I have had published. The first piece I wrote was a birthday present for a very special friend. I have been writing poetry and philosophy for two years now. My inspiration comes for people in need of healing in many forms.

This poem was inspired by a meditation on any kind of footwear. I immediately thought of a pair of moccasins, although I didn't actually see them. The rest just followed in about two minutes flat, although it did take a bit longer than that to put into words, later on.

The young Indian brave was fleet of foot as he ran along the river bank.
The lush green grass made a soft carpet for his feet.

A fish caught from the stream was his repast and a tree served as his back rest and support whilst he sat and contemplated life.

A snow-topped mountain painted the horizon in the distance.
A dark green forest nestled in the valley below whilst the river gently
meandered.

The sky was of the deepest blue and the sun shone brightly.
Bird songs filled the air punctuated by the occasional 'plop' of an
inquisitive fish.

Animals of the forest ventured forth with no feeling of apprehension or danger. They are used to the company of the man with stillness in him.

The beauty of the sights and sounds fill his heart with unbounded love for all, whilst he unconsciously contributes to the wholeness of the picture.

Wisdom can come from blending with the peace and joy of nature. Taking time to be at one with the earth as God made it. Quietness will teach much if you let it.

Dolly Little

The City

How we loved the salt sea air. How we loved
To watch the sea as it washed and cleansed
The smooth shore. Our Mother we called her.
The waves would climb and crash and billow
Ever upwards like horses leaping and dancing.

It was such a beautiful city.
At midday the city shone whiter than the foam.
Then, ablaze in the setting sun, she would gaze
Warm and tranquil, like a folding rose.

Because the king was peaceful and strong for so long,
As the salt spray bleached and clung to the houses
So that they sparkled like diamonds,
We grew complacent, satisfied.
When the youngest son brought home his bride,
How we loved her, we saw the sea personified.

This island is small, it looks to the west,
As our city did.
The shore is straight and sure
Strewn by giant boulders hidden by the waves
So it can never be crushed to a crescent moon
Like the old harbour.

We still watch the sea and believe
The father and mother are united in love.
The horses still prance and dance on the shore.
As they used to.

This island is hard to reach, so far.
It is hard to harm us here. The old gods were angry.
The new perplexed, though the light lived on.

We will always remember our beautiful, folding rose.
Inspired by the sun, changed to a roaring, red furnace.
Fused by the fear of those who refuse to understand, or love.
But now thank God, now, we have found a home again.

Cejayo Farrell

Notes

I am a widow and have one son, a partner in a firm of solicitors, and one daughter, who works in the City Treasurer's Office. I was born in Tunstall, Stoke-on-Trent, not far from Clarice Cliff, and still live in the Potteries, not many miles from Stanley Matthews.

Suitably attired, my sister and I performed *We're Dowagers from Ealing*, as a duo, in Town Halls, Church Halls and at charity shows. My main hobby is painting and I have had pictures accepted by the Open Art Exhibition and exhibited in the museum in Hanley, Stoke-on-Trent. I have sold many pictures on different subjects but I love trees. In my youth I designed pottery - tea ware - painting patterns.

A Dowager From Ealing

I'm a dowager from Ealing, so frustrated, and revealing
The kind of things that life is all about.
I've finished with the 'fellas' and I've taken to 'spirellas'
Now I'm through with babies, I've got gout!
Everything I've got's been lifted, slapped and tickled, or been shifted
Thru the years - I feel it can't have been in vain.
I've had gentlemen admirers, sable stoles and flash tiaras.
What I've done, I know, I'd love to do again!
Taken tea with Lady Chumley, I've done Ascot, I've done Henley
Sailed in Aristotle's yacht, to name a few!
I've been dressed in haute couture, by Balkan, and many more.
Among the flowers with Paul Getty, down at Kew.
But the world has changed a lot, all our ethics gone to pot.
The future is for ladies and for tramps!
I've had my kicks and thrills, be it good or be it ill.
Now I'd even get a high from
Green Shield Stamps!

M C Heath

Tunnel Vision

Notes

I was brought up and educated on the coast of Fife and in Edinburgh. After teaching there and in Glasgow, I was head teacher of a small school in Perthshire until my retirement, and was recently widowed.

My poem was inspired by harrowing news items of war and death, and was written for a friend who shares with me a love of music, poetry and literature, and a deep concern for the present state of the world, as we approach the millennium.

I am now sub-editor and columnist of our award-winning local newspaper, The Villagers.

My eyes look terrible. In the looking-glass
Their mirror image stares back, blank, blear
And wild with weeping.
Hearts and hopes like mirrors, all shattered
In war and death, history recollected.
Look into my eyes. Do you see
Reflections of man's folly?
Image on image, reflected and reflected
A tunnel of glass, darkened, blood-spattered
Bores in my brain.
Friend and enemy pass through. Pain and fear,
Army on army. I see their spirits pass.

Thea Matyjasek

Notes

I live in a village in Cambridgeshire with a dog, two cats and a husband.

I started writing poetry in September 1996, and get my inspiration for my poems from my love of nature. I also enjoy gardening and reading.

The Spider and the Ladybird

The spider spins his silvery web
With its intricate pattern of gossamer thread.
He sits in the middle and awaits his prey
Patience is needed, but no luck today.

The next day comes and he's still there
Sat in the middle of his wondrous lair.
His eyes wide open and his wits alert
A ladybird comes, but she's just a flirt.

She'll not enter his den, she knows how it ends,
She's seen it before with many of her friends,
But the spider smiles as he sits in his lure.
One day, soon, he'll catch her for sure.

Deirdre O'Connor-Long

226

Notes

I live in Hornchurch, Essex and am employed as Health Liaison Officer for a Trust at a local hospital. I have a grown-up family and five grandchildren who actually inspired one of my poems.

I have no previous writing experience and, although I have put words together in my mind since I was a child, it is only recently that I began to put the words to paper.

I cannot order myself to compose a poem; I will be in a certain situation or at a location, looking at a painting or reading a book, smell a certain perfume (I could go on and on) and the words are there in my head. My poetry then flows onto paper.

I adore art galleries, am at my happiest walking in the countryside and visiting locations steeped in history. I visited Clare Priory on a very cold, gloomy day. I was completely alone and as I walked, slowly, round the grounds I felt the history of the place and imagined ghostly images floating round the remaining walls, which were covered in Virginia creeper. Words were suddenly in my head and I had to write them down, there and then.

Clare Priory

Floating, whispering, kissing leaves
of coppice hidden deep
gossamer shroud, encircling walls
hovering over hallowed ground

Transparent fingers stroking
russet ivy, clinging, entwining
decaying, crumbling stone
caressing mound and sepulchre.

Jean Dunn

Notes

Fredric A Walsh was born and reared in Liverpool at the outbreak of World War Two. Having travelled widely in his career he has settled in Worcester where he runs a craft business with his partner.

His first foray into imaginative writing was when he dreamed up stories to tell to his two daughters at bedtime. The intervening years did not allow time to devote to writing until recently and he now has plans to catch up.

His main inspiration comes from everyday life with a particular leaning to the great outdoors.

Horizon's Call, however, is his reflection on a long hard road to middle age.

Horizon's Call

In all needs man must when in despair
Find solace and rectitude on God's own air
Do not in hours sad rely on laurels past
Nor pray for help on whims not built to last
Take strength to right the sorrows of unwitting wrongs
And strive toward the sound of happy songs
If those hills of life in their tangent do offer strain
Keep all effort and on God's hand rely again
With one thought do hold your vision of a future life
That sings of praise and comfort in absenting strife
And when you reach that seeming distant plane
Remember once that others need your gain
To hold a hand when yours is pain indeed
Will sow forever sure that rightful seed.

Fredric A Walsh

An Abecedarian Verse

Notes

I was born in Yorkshire and am a retired SRN. I have three daughters and one grandson.

I have been writing poetry for a long time and have had five other poems accepted. My poems concern both my family and friends; events of all kinds inspire me.

I like to garden, growing both flowers and vegetables. I love reading, crosswords, pressed flower pictures, tapestry, embroidery and cooking.

A bird fluttered down but
Before reaching the ground
Came to the flowering cherry tree.
Down came a host of petals
Each shaded pink and each ready to
Fall upon the green grass or to
Go floating upon the clear water -
Hiding the myriad tadpoles
In the small garden pool.
Just then a squirrel approached,
Keen eyes on the alert -
Looking here and there -
Making swift dashes for
Nuts scattered on the lawn.
Overhead a magpie squawks
Plummeting down to a tall conifer
Quaking in the blustery wind.
Round the nut holders blue and coal tits,
Sparrows and green finches foregather -
Taking turns to peck - then flying
Under the tree before
Veering and seeking the odd fallen nut;
Watchful as ever for
X - the unknown factor - a predator?
Yea - a furry feline slinking along
Zapping the grounded birds.

Ada M Witheridge

Notes

This was written for Dr Rupa Wickramaratne, from Sri Lanka, who did her PhD with me at Imperial College, London.

I am author or co-author of books on wine and beer judging, genetics, how to write about biology, English for technology, English standards of UK undergraduates and of young entrants to industry and commerce. I also write short stories.

Tears of Time

'When I reach thirty,' Rupa said,
'Whole lakes of tears I'll freely shed.
And all the earth shall turn to mud
Beneath this lachrymosal flood!'

But now a further year has passed,
Will this birthday's flow be vast?
Or will matureness stand the strain
And dry those lovely eyes again?

Bernard Lamb

Notes

To my eldest granddaughter, to celebrate her eighteenth birthday.

My Prittlewell-gel, Louise

I saw her in a Rochford ward
A baby sweet and fair.
I saw her first steps, with her walking frame,
A toddler outside care.
She flew the vault and skimmed the bars
Somersaulted the balance beam with ease.
'Twas not a grander babe than her
My Prittlewell-gel, Louise!

I saw her run cross-country fields,
Down dales, cross muddy streams.
I saw her sprint; race track events.
The darling of my dreams!
She long-jumped, with the winning best,
Her teams were wholly pleased!
There's not a grander girl than her
She's a pretty-swell, Louise!

I saw her schooling at open days,
Her work was up to measure.
I saw and heard her music play,
A tune for saints, to treasure.
Her college work is ahead her now
Her future there to seize!
There's nay a promising beauty-belle
Than my protégé, Louise!

I've seen her spring from babe to teens
She's daintily aspiring.
With purpose, passion and family pride
Her presence the most admiring.
My hopes are hers, to foster - to see?
There's not a better person - for she
Is my wonder-girl, Louise!

Ron Amato

Notes

I live in Germany as my Dad is in the forces. I attend Windsor school where I am currently studying for my GCSE's.

This is my first piece of work I have had published, which both myself and my family are very proud of, and, hopefully it won't be my last.

I just want to say thanks to everyone who has helped me get into the pages of this book.

The Coming War

They knew it was coming . . .

All around the forest floor,
Creatures sheltered from the coming war.
They had seen the distant, murderous clouds,
And now sought to hide beneath their shrouds.

A sighing wind promised storms asunder,
Slashing rain and roaring thunder,
Then speeding winds humbled the trees,
And the shivering branches were an image of the seas.

Lightning leapt from the angry, brooding clouds,
The thunder roared and announced that it was proud,
Of the heated death it escorted through the sky,
Leaving behind pain and anguished cries.

The storm beat down, hour after hour,
Destroying the forest with its almighty power.
But it finally ended, leaving only forlorn stars,
With the distant sound of thunder, echoing from afar . . .

And all around the forest floor,
Creatures emerged from the finished war.
They had survived the murderous storm,
And now they waited for the coming dawn.

Dawn Feltoe (15)

The Ghost of Hallowe'en

Notes

I was born and have lived my life in Braintree, a small market town in Essex. I worked for a local manufacturing company for over twenty years, until it closed, and have worked for the local authority for the last eight years.

I started writing poetry many years ago, but the first poem I have had published was earlier this year, twenty years after I had first written it. Since then, I have had four more poems accepted for publication, including this one. My ambition for the future is to have a book of my own poetry published.

The mist hung over the river
On a cold October night
As we ventured down the narrow lane
There wasn't a creature in sight

The roadway was becoming quite slippery
With frost forming on the ground
And apart from the flowing river
There was no other sound

As we walked along in silence
Our breath hung on the air
With the fog becoming much denser
It formed moisture on our hair

Suddenly footsteps were heard in the distance
Giving us both a terrible fright
Gathering speed we hurried along
Wondering who was out on such a night

The footsteps became much closer
Then suddenly something touched my arm
So startled and afraid to see
I hoped we would come to no harm

I turned and looked in amazement
There was nobody to be seen
Was it just a trick of the imagination
Or the Ghost of Hallowe'en.

Linda A Brown

Notes

As soon as I knew my alphabet and could form a few words I wanted to write, first stories (fairy tales) and then verses. I have always written for my own pleasure and for friends who clamoured for more. My first story (fairy) was written just before my seventh birthday, for friends at school.

I took care that no grown-ups saw my efforts - I thought reprimands might be in the offing. Thus I proceeded through all my schooldays, until I left school at 14 (in March 1914). I attended a course of business training for two years then went out to 'business' as a shorthand typist. I did not like it - a very cramped office shared with the secretary and a boss who swore. I left there after five weeks - took Friday off and found a job where a 'boy' was wanted. I outdid any office boy they had previously had and stayed there for over 12 years, marrying one of HM Senior Service sailors. Our marriage lasted until his death, aged 86, in 1982.

I became a temp and stayed in one temporary job for 19½ years, leaving at the age of 74¾ in 1974, because of redundancy. Had I joined the staff as I was implored to do many times, I would have had a state pension of my own - but I did not think it quite right to take a full-time job with a home and family to care for.

I have 3 daughters and 1 son, 5 grandchildren and 2 great grandchildren. I wish there were more!

I am interested in reading, writing, the arts, children and elderly persons. I do not care for sports but like to watch the feats of others, usually on TV. I do not watch much otherwise - too much sex, violence and nonsense! I'm six months older than the lovely Queen Mother and am old fashioned!

Drifting

I feel that I am drifting, drifting,
Yet know not where I go
Encushioned in safe and gentle arms
Above the earth below.

Drifting in effortless movement
I feel I don't belong
To earth's pulsating human crowd
This noisy, unheeding throng.

So I drift in idle wonder
In safe and warm embrace
Viewing from somewhere far away
This tide in time and space.

Then as I go wildly drifting
O'er this world far above
Compassionate prayers envelop me
For huge downpours of love.

B F Smyth

Notes

My name is James Martin Butler, I am 21 and live in Birmingham with my two sisters, Catherine and Bernadette, and my recently widowed mother, Josephine.

I have spent time at Drama School and I intend to study an English degree at University.

On a trip to Europe, my friend Richard and I were on a train bound for Athens; aboard, I met a beautiful Danish girl called Christina. After two wonderful days in Athens we parted paths. It was on a train from Dover to London, in a melancholy mood, that I was inspired to write the poem, about her.

Dedicated to Christina Gade.

Her

Her love is like an idyllic portrait of clouds,
Once I glare into those passionate blue skies
My heart fills with song, which shrieks aloud,
So I pray to the Lord that our love never dies.

Dance a jolly dance in the street with my love,
Watch, as her flaxen, flaxen hair falls beneath her face,
We sense the magic of the air with the stars above,
She is perfect to the touch, like the finest of lace.

So why? oh why? the afflictions of life!
I philosophise each day, I philosophise each night.
Christina, you have left me, and it feels like someone is turning a knife.
Like an angel has wings, I wish you had flight.

So I could take you to be my beautiful wife
Through the progression of time, and beyond both our lives.

James M Butler

Notes

Lorraine Ellen Willson was born in 1955, in London. She is now a purchasing officer and lives in Kent, with John, her long term partner, and two cats, Arnie and Rufus.

She plays in North Kent Quiz League and was a keen horse rider until a fall resulted in a broken spine. She now risks the thrills of a Susuki 750 motor bike. She has travelled to the Far East, America and Egypt and is now planning a trip to Africa.

Poetry writing began at school and in 1995, a first novel, Punch and Judy, was finished, hopefully, to be published.

This poem was inspired when, as a child, Lorraine watched the Grand National and learnt what the word 'destroyed' meant.

The poem is dedicated to the memory of Molly, my best friend.

The 'Dead' Cert

This is it then, my fame and future done
I'm lying in a muddy field, looking at a gun.
I'd heard about the National, my entry a dead cert,
That was before I fell today, and they cannot mend my hurt.
I suppose I should be grateful
As death goes mine will be quick
A single bullet to the head,
A jerk, perhaps a kick.
The knacker's van I know is near,
The smell of death is strong.
The men all gathered around me
Say it's my fault, I took it wrong.
It must be time I reckon,
The screens are put in place,
To hide me from the punters,
Who bet on me this race.
They tear their tickets in disgust
Paper flutters in the breeze
As the vet kneels down beside me
To inspect my shattered knees.
He shakes his head so slowly
As he rises to his feet
A fleeting pat upon my neck
I know I'm done-for meat.
I wonder what will happen,
When I'm hauled up on the van
Will they take me to the kennels.
Or will I end up in a can?
Beef and liver, or kidney and heart
Will I end up as a treat,
For some old lady's pampered dog
That gets more than her to eat.
This is it I reckon, the gun's against my head,
He's no good to me, he'll not race again
That's what my owner said.
The finger's on the trigger
A voice shouts 'come on man, look smart'
'Let's get this bloody mess cleared up.
The 3.30's about to start.'

L E Willson

Notes

I am 55 years old and have been married for 34 years. I have two grown up children and four beautiful grandchildren.

My hobbies include: music (an obsession), literature (also an obsession), playing classical guitar, painting (mostly water colour), sketching, photography, long walks and my grandchildren (also an obsession).

The poem came about as a result of walking past the playground of a park but not, as the poem implies, one that my children had played upon. It was actually one that I myself played on when I was about eleven years old, so the shade in the shadows is myself.

Someone, Something

A silent roundabout turning in an empty park
Chases yesterday's shadows through the windy dark
Their footsteps are just the rustle of dried-out leaves.
'Catch me! Catch me if you can!'
Was that the wind?
'Catch me if you can!' I thought I heard someone call across the park
Then someone, something, touched me in the dark.

Sand flows into the footprint of a child
As if a foot had but recent stood there
The edges crumble and begin to break
And a ghostly giggle, skipping through the air
Running through the bushes and the trees
Fades to become a dog's far-distant bark
But someone, something, touched me in the dark.

The swing's chains rattle, as if someone took a seat
I hear a scream come from the skelter slide
My dog comes whimpering to my feet
As if to say, 'Master! Someone in the darkness hides!'

Yes. Someone in the darkness hides
It is the shadows of my children three
Laughing. Giggling. Playing in the past
Calling 'Come and play!' to children yet to be
And, though memories may seem to fade away
On occasions, such as this, a voice calls hark
And someone, something, touches in the dark.

Bryan Sefton

Why Does Nobody Call?

Down by the river is my estate
With its pathways and trees so tall
It's a place where residents can often be heard saying
'Why does nobody call?'

It's a strange place here,
Maybe a year or so that I came
I didn't want to move from my former home
but I had to come just the same

It started fine when family and friends
Came by to help with the garden
But one by one they failed to show up
With no hint of a prayer or a pardon
Why does nobody call?

My wife is a local but we've had a divorce
She resides down the road by the church
She never visits just lays in wait for our son
They think I left them both in the lurch

Aunt Flo came with flowers just yesterday
Strutting the path full of life
I thought that maybe she was calling on me
But she turned off to visit my wife
Why does nobody call?

The winters are the worst down here by the river
No carols or kings at Yule Tide
Family and friends forget as in summer
The place where I now abide

But if you should be passing
Please pay me a visit
Or come over by the fence and just wave
The address?
Oh, yes of course . . . it's down by the river
The cemetery, in a box called the grave.
Why does nobody call?

Ray Eldridge

Shady

This grizzly figure
Watches on
Pale corpse stares back
Her eyes - half closed,
Her hair - shabby.
Dry skin patches
Peeling - unaware.
The mouth - untouchable,
Sleep grows like cataract.
Midnight dribble
Now dried up.
Her mind empty
She moves away.

Saiqa Hussain

Notes

I was born in Somerset in 1946, my mother is Marion Billett, my father is deceased. I married Roger Stephen Moseley in 1977: we have a daughter, Sally Ann. I was educated at Ellesmere Port Grammar School and Chester College of Further Education. I worked as a specialised plant and shrub specialist for eleven years, until developing ME, three years ago.

I was awarded the Editor's Choice Award for Outstanding Achievement for Poetry, with a piece entitled *I Ask Why*, published in the anthology, Voices on the Wind (1996). Many of my poems have been published in the Clarion, the Bournemouth Evening Echo and the Berrynarbor Newsletter.

I find my inspiration from subjects and incidents that I feel very strongly about. *Ode to Beacon Hill, I Ask Why* and *Night-time Mania* were written after a three year battle to prevent a landfill site on our doorsteps for the next twenty two years - sadly we lost. Hence, *Ode to Beacon Hill*, portraying the impact this horrendous proposal will have on the environment and our children's future.

My mother lives in Sterridge Valley, North Devon, and the beauty and friendliness of all around her inspired me to write *My Family in the Valley*.

I enjoy reading poetry but am not inspired by other writers. My constant companion is Lottie, my Cavalier King Charles spaniel - an exception to her noble breed, hence my poem, *Royalty Indeed*.

I write poems for people who have lost pets, and put them into cards. I thank my dad, he taught me about love and the good in life; and from my heart I wonder and look at the beauty of the land God gave us.

Inspired

It's early morning I lie in bed
Jumbled words whirl inside my head.
What are they saying, what do they mean?
Was I asleep or was it a dream
My body cries out I am so tired
But my unconscious mind has become inspired -
To write a poem for you

Pick up paper, pen by bed
What were those words inside my head
I cannot think now I'm awake
Jotted words on paper no sense do make
Back to sleep, I am so tired
As I slip away my unconscious mind inspired -
To dream a poem for you.

A M Moseley

Notes

I am a widow, retired and living alone in a warden-controlled flat, in Hampshire.

I attended a creative writing course and had two poems published in their magazine, and two poems in the local parish magazine.

My hobbies are painting and writing. My interest in writing poetry began at school, in English lessons. Things that inspire me are nature, the sea and especially happy memories and times of sadness.

My inspiration for this particular poem came when I saw the sun shining on the grass, wet with dew, in my garden.

Early Morning

Rainbows, glistening in the grass,
Dancing in the dew on each bending blade,
The sun releasing each spectral shade
Briefly, to pass

In ever-changing broken light
Across my lush untended lawn,
A verdant setting bejewelled at dawn
Iridescent, bright;

This phenomenon of dew and light
Held my gaze 'til drifting cloud
Veiled the sun with silver shroud
And gave the rainbows flight.

M M Mose

Notes

I am 59 years old, have four children and three grand-children. I work as a book-keeper and live in Chelsea.

I have had eighty poems accepted for publication in anthologies in the last fourteen months. I have won three runners-up prizes in poetry competitions.

I am a spiritual healer and am devoted to animal, human and planet rights, and to housing and feeding everything on this earth in the way he/she/it wants to be housed and fed.

My hobbies are: my friends, reading, theatre, opera, ballet, etc.

I started writing in late 1987, when I was temporarily out of work. Anything inspires me, from a rose to a rainbow or a beautiful picture - I also write protest poems about abuses of all kinds.

The inspiration for this poem was the pollution all around us, and the effect it has, and will have, on all forms of life. Also the lack of interest most people have in the state of the world.

Contamination

They made us all use smokeless fuel
so the air we breathed was fresh,
but now it's filled with pollutants
and we're trapped inside its mesh.

We inhale its poisons day by day
when we work, or play, or shop,
and our children suffer more than us,
for *them* - it's got to stop.

For we are really responsible,
we're the wise ones, so we think,
then why don't we make our Governments
get rid of this awful stink?

Do we really take an interest?
Do we honestly want to know?
Let's pretend it doesn't happen
then perhaps the threat will go.

Daf Richards

Notes

The Cycle

This poem is inspired by spring, the spark-plug of the seasons, and explores cycles, which I have always found fascinating.

At first glance, the human life cycle stands out, but is highlighted and reinforced by the cycle of seasons and of weather, the cycle of rest and of play and the cycle of joy and tears.

Summer sweet to winter frail,
Hears zephyr sigh and mistral wail.
The years leapt past the child of days,
With formless words of love and praise.

Duties summon but games will call,
And tasks forgotten left to fall.
The girl will learn to laugh and sing
And help gather the harvest in.

Trials o'ercome and joy bring tears
They add their depth to all her years.
The woman learns to steady hands
And wonders of her life and plans.

Summer sweet to winter frail
Have wound a glad and solemn tale.
With every beat her babe hears love
And wonders what she's thinking of.

Lynn French

Notes

I'm 23 years of age and live in Leicestershire. I have been writing poems for the past year and have managed to complete seventy.

Recently, I have had a poem published with The International Library of Poets.

Writing poems seemed the natural thing to do and now it has become a way of life.

HIV + (Now Until Then) was put together in 1995, and was inspired by a television programme about Aids and how people are trying to live with it.

I dedicate this to all those people and my heart goes out to them.

HIV + (Now Until Then)

Everyone seems to be dropping like flies,
Maybe they all thought it was lies.
Infested with the wretched disease,
They've no chance to live at ease.

Do they feel it living in their veins
Or in their hearts - maybe the same.
How we wish they could have a second
Chance, but it's not to be, try to enhance.

A feeling of guilt, but why should it be,
'Cos it's all to do with them - it's not me.

The time will come, a time to heal, but
For now until then it's all so real.

M Haffner

The Tree at Selbourne

Notes

Selbourne is a village in Hampshire, made famous by the curate, Gilbert White, who wrote a book about the local flora and fauna of one small area there, known as The Hangar.

For many hundred years the old yew stood
'Twixt vicarage and church, shadowed by hilly wood
How many young sweethearts had made their vows
Beneath the tented shelter of its heavy boughs?
How many merry marriage parties crossed its path
With eager steps and happy, loving laugh?
How many babies, brought to have the blessing of a Christian name
Carried to the church by doting parents came?
And at the last, with slow and solemn tread
How many bearers carried past their dead?
The life of puny man drifts idly by
Under the massive yew tree's watchful eye!
Secure and steadfast, clasping tight the earth,
With roots set deep, spread wider than its girth.

Then came the day a great wind ripped apart the land
And swathes of trees were felled, as with a mighty hand.
Roofs torn off houses, walls and fences smashed,
Cars tossed into the air and crashed.
But surely not this dear and ancient tree
Who, like a friend, we sometimes call and see.
Yet there before us - thanks to TV's modern magic
We saw our tree, uprooted, bare and tragic
An ancient soldier, stripped of dignity,
With boughs chopped off - was this our lovely tree?
A hole was made by crowds of men around.
They'd hired a crane to drop it in the ground!

We mourned his loss, yet dared not see his grave
But hoped that he might live, he was so brave.
Our casual friendship lasted more than sixty years
Yet should a tree be cause for human tears?

Two years passed by before we went to see
Just what had happened to our mighty tree.
The torn and battered trunk showed signs of twiggy green,
Life springing from the love and care so clearly seen
In a simple card for all to note as they might pass,
'Tree convalescing - Please Keep Off The Grass'

We felt our hopes were shattered when we heard the tree had died
Yet now new life is springing from the sapling of its shattered side.

Beryl Preston

The Famous Lion

Notes

I am nine years old and started writing poetry, along with elocution, which was two years ago.

My hobbies include: lots of sport, drawing and writing.

My inspiration to write comes with boredom.

The director says,
'We need a real lion,
For the Wizard of Oz.
One with a curly mane,
But surely a lion can't have fame.
One with a brain,
But not a brain in pain.'

'One with mighty claws,
One with hard paws.
One with teeth so sharp,
To sing while a lady plays the harp.
A strong voice that makes the windows break,
Are we really making, the house of fame.'

Rachel Plant (9)

The World's Kind of People

Notes

I am sixty four, married with two children and live in Bromley, Kent. My very first poem was written in 1943, titled *The Poppys*.

Within the last two years, encouraged by my wife and family, I sent poems for publishing, and have now had some fourteen poems accepted for publication.

The World's Kind of People is dedicated to members of my local church, St Mary's, Orpington, who, to me, represent many within the church and outside, who give their time to the local community and nations of the world.

The world's kind of people.
Take time to care
Have time to share
The world's kind of people.

The world's kind of people.
Of different race and creed.
Bring medicine, blankets.
Water and seed.

The world's kind of people.
Give hope.
Where there is despair.
Love.
When there is hatred.
They show they care.

The world's kind of people.
Walk Ben Nevis for sponsored coin.
Take clothes to Croatia, Angola.
And dangerous convoys join.

The world's kind of people.
John, Lynda, Barbara, Dot.
Give their time for others.
Their own gifts.
They share a lot.

The world's kind of people.
Priests of many faiths.
Are soldiers fighting greed.
Forever fighting suffering.
It is their mustard seed.

The world's kind of people.
Forget about the strife.
Their time is sometimes taken.
With a cherished life.

The world's kind of people.
Are the world's to embrace.
For what they give to nations.
They have a special place.
The world's kind of people.

Frederick Seymour

Notes

I am 46 years old, married with three children and live in Inverness, Scotland. I work as a care assistant in a hostel for vulnerable and homeless people, and my wife works as a nursing auxiliary.

I first started writing to celebrate special occasions, but just over a year ago, I began writing poetry as a serious hobby. My youngest son, Martin (12), sometimes adds his compositions to my collection. This is the first poem I have had printed. It was written during half an hour of intense peace and quiet!

Peace and Quiet

Peace and quiet -
More precious than sleep,
Flowing through your nerves and muscles,
Tingling all over, buzzing deep.

A refuge from chaos -
A break in the noise and rush,
Being something like thick foliage,
Creating a shade, creating a hush.

Soothing vibrations -
Coming from the after-hum,
Bringing you in sympathy with nothingness,
Leaving you painless, leaving you numb.

A short interlude -
A few moments of escape,
Interrupting the busy life,
Giving it meaning, giving it shape.

Paul Heinowski

Void

Restlessly I wander, like a lost soul,
That rattles angrily the grey birch branches,
And snatches the last few leaves from its twigs.
Sending every leaf shivering downward.
Down to the lifeless earth,
Asleep in autumnal bliss.
I shall not awake the earth's silent sleep,
But ever so lightly tread,
And wait impatiently until spring.

Geraldine Hampson

Notes

I am a 75 year old widow, a retired nurse tutor with a grown-up family; I live in Worthing.

I started writing poetry seriously, after moving down here three and a half years ago. Since when, I have had thirteen poems published in anthologies compiled by Anchor Press, and one with The International Society of Poets.

Living by the sea, with access to the South Downs, I find nature in all her phases inspirational. I have a strong religious faith and am a practising member of the Church of England.

My hobbies are reading, listening to music, embroidery (cross stitch), and relaxing with my many friends.

Sonnet to Summer

When summer spreads her mantle on the ground
The whole wide world of nature comes alive.
Bright golden days with cloudless skies abound
Causing dejected spirits to revive.
The hedgerow rich with meadowsweet and rose
Pours incense-perfumed fragrance on the air.
Each sun-drenched shore, a precious gift bestows
On children as they laugh and frolic there.
The dreary town, with dank polluted street
Attempts to lift its jaded eyes above
In flower-decked park, where shy young couples meet
And pledge to each their everlasting love.
And in my heart there blooms sweet thoughts of you
To help me see chill winter's greyness through.

Elsie Anderson

The Meteor

November evening on the soft brown Cornish sand;
November starlight as we wandered hand in hand;
Cool autumn breezes and the murmur of the sea
And a girl who meant all heaven and the world to me.

Long sandy coastline on the shore of Perranporth;
Great Atlantic rollers coming coastwards from the north;
Stars in the heavens and a cloudless, open sky,
Memory of that night of beauty shall not ever die.

Hushed were our voices as our hearts whispered love
And we lifted up our eyes to the starry dome above;
And even as we gazed, there appeared a wondrous sight
As a meteor through the heavens flashed its brilliance on the night.

Gone in an instant but remembered through the years,
Lighting up the darkness in the valley of our tears;
For in that very moment I was sure that we were one,
I knew that life for you and me had really just begun.

And every time across the sky I see a shooting star,
Speeding on its wayward path from unknown realms afar,
I dream of a time when a girl and I went forth
On a peaceful autumn evening on the shore of Perranporth.

Donald MacColl

Notes

I am 63 years old, married, retired and living in West Yorkshire. I started writing about twenty five years ago. Until now, I have never had anything published due to the fact that I wrote solely for my own amusement, and never considered the idea of publication.

This particular poem was written, among others, during a period of searching for 'answers' following the sudden and unexplained death of my eldest son, which resulted in a disillusionment with the church as a whole. Hence, the *Questions*!

My interests mainly consist of reading and walking, and the inspiration for my writing usually comes from personal experiences both serious and humorous.

Questions

Great holy piles by God-fearing hand,
were built in scores throughout our land.
To gather in His erring sheep
and protect them outside castle keep.
Canterbury, Salisbury and at York,
Great houses for the 'holy talk'
thrust pointed fingers to the sky.
What mean they now to you and I?

Do they mean that God's alive?
Should we crowd like bees to hive?
Do we need their sanctuary?
Do they help us - you and me?
No! Now we only stand and gawp
as massive timbers creak and warp.
Their stones dissolve to dust away
and bishops pray for us to pay.

Why do we try to save these great
massive heaps of stone and slate?
Surely not for our benefit,
for we no more on Sunday sit
in oak pews to hear the word
or send our prayers like fleet-winged bird
soaring far into the sky,
to reach the ears of God on high.

Are they really our heritage
these reminders of a Christian age?
An age that's gone - maybe for good
to return not to this nation's blood.
Why not now face cold hard fact,
and maybe do one Christian act?
Save time and money - let them fall,
instead let's make a home for all!

Philip Kapp

252

The Hypochondriac

Liv Holst Mitchell was born and educated in Norway. After being brought up in Trondheim, her family then moved to Oslo, where, after various temporary positions, she trained as a wireless operator and began her career in the radio room on board a merchant naval vessel.

She first arrived in London in 1954 and was later to marry Andrew Mitchell and settle in Britain permanently. Her daughter, Katrina, was born in 1965 and her son, Andrew, in 1969.

Among her many activities, Liv has studied with the Open University, obtaining a BA (Hons) in 1992. Her other interests include playing classical guitar and piano. She first began writing poetry privately as a child, and the recent death of her husband has spurred her on to write several pieces.

The Hypochondriac was partly inspired by her brother-in-law, Jack.

As he wakes every morning
his first thought is this
Where do I feel bad today?
Is it the stomach
is the heart beat right
or did I drink too much wine
last night?
My head is definitely sore
my liver's complaining
Why, this sudden pain
in my chest and the rest
I feel stiff all over
My veins are hurting
they seem to explode
my heart is pounding
do I look all right?
Dashing to the mirror
looking aghast
yesterday's person
is now in his last
throes of going, and going for good
That bluish pallor
those sunken eyes
There's no way he can last
I must phone my doctor
he must understand
But, what is the point
I know my body so much better than he
the odd swelling here
the missing heart beat there
But I need my pills for this and that
and maybe an unsatisfactory chat
He can at least give me that

One day he will be sorry
that doctor of mine
that he didn't listen
to my woes and whine
And when I have gone
it is possible too
that he realises
all I told him was true

L R Mitchell

Notes

This poem was written for a person who was grieving for a 'special someone' who had died, but on reading it from a different aspect, it could apply to a lost love. To someone we have loved but circumstances have parted. There must have been a lot of happiness given, to feel such pain.

I'm an ordinary person, 50 plus, with two grown-up sons and I'm a granny. Life doesn't begin at 40. It begins when you let the fear of 'I can't' go to 'let's try and see what happens'. So, let your soul soar free!

Reach For the Stars

Reach for the stars
Accept nothing less.
They're set in dark velvet
Where our thoughts are all met.
Through the open door
Send your love on
To those gone before.

When your life was empty
You stood deep alone.
Wondered, how could this be,
'Why is there no one
To really love me?'
All that I wanted
Was a warm hand in mine.
A heart that said;
'I'll love you, till the end of time.'

Experience has taught me
The values of life.
Not money or houses
Which though give delight.
It's a pair of warm eyes
That glow, with that special light.

Let the pain subside,
Let my soul soar free.
Let me reach for the stars
And be, really me.

Myrna M Bailey

Notes

Steph Greenwood is 19 and is currently in the first year of a teacher training degree. She took a year out between finishing her A levels and going to University to spend 8 months working as a volunteer teacher in an underprivileged rural school in Uganda.

The Four Horsemen was written before she left England and she only had a media image of Africa; Uganda was not as she expected. There is disease and death but no famine and more love and peace than hate and war; everyone should experience that.

The Four Horsemen

Pestilence, War, Famine and Death,
Around the world every day.
Four horsemen of the Apocalypse,
Affect us all in a different way.

Disease spreads, not like water or fire
But a rumour that needs to be known.
Drugs are defeated and Media manifests,
A dying child's face to the world is shown.

World-wide wisdom results in war,
Dousing Earth in Fear, Greed and Hate.
Peace process to diplomatic deal,
For thousands, unfairly, it's already too late.

Through destitution people starve and die,
No hope of food, they soon become weak.
Sickly babes become skin-covered skeletons
Crying in hunger, too ill to speak.

A mother is sick, her children surround her,
In a hospital bed she's waiting to die.
No Third World country with no NHS,
In countries like ours, we must ask, 'Why?'

Steph Greenwood

Notes

I was born in Dublin in the sixties and have been living in England for three years, whilst pursuing a nursing career in Bath. The Phoenix Park is one of the largest parks in the world, spanning some 1,752 acres. The park was established as a wild deer park by the Duke of Ormond in 1662.

It is home to the fox, badger, Irish stoat, red and grey squirrels, as well as herds of wild deer. The Oakwood, Ancient Oak and Evergreen Oak are some of the many varieties of trees there.

The park was very much part of my childhood and adolescent years. It was a place my father brought the family on Sunday afternoons for walks and he often made us swings with ropes tied over branches. Later it became a place for solitude and mediation during my teenage years and it was here that I met my first love.

Love in the Phoenix is the first poem I have had published.

Love in the Phoenix

Eighteen summers have gone by and I still remember him who my soul
loved
upon whose breast lay my head in rest, we talked of things gone by and
things to come
but did not speak of where we lay in each other's future plans.

Beneath the shade of leafy tree we would sit
on that side of the ravine which we'd come to call
'the dark side of the moon'
and watch the fading light, as the darkness crept in.

And there we'd while away an hour or two.
Enjoy the solace of those summer eves.
Enjoy the stroke of hand on long dark hair
on brow, on face, on lips, the warm sweet taste of kiss.

At half past ten we'd rise to walk
across that moonlit park
between the ghostly trees which loomed against the midnight blue of sky.
Stopping to look over the 'Furry Glen'
to see the light of moon upon the lake and hear the sound of drake and
duck
resting in its darkened banks.

Going on home we'd sometime run
laughing our way up that hill,
and at the corner, have our final smoke and joke
we talked of things we'd done and things to come.
Saying those goodbyes he'd promise we would meet next time
but never said when that time would be,
and I, lived for the possibility.

Tessa Merriman

Notes

A married housewife with two grown-up children, I have written poetry since my teens, but without thinking of publishing until now.

Literature and nature are my greatest interests and coupled with a rural life, help create my source of inspiration.

Birds

Shelley wrote to the lark,
Oh listen to it - hark.
Hardy told of the thrush
Which made the senses rush.

Poe told of a raven dark
That cried 'Nevermore' so stark.
Rossetti's raven did croak
'Death' from the bough of an oak.

Mary Smith

Notes

R W Kinkaid was a product
designer, inventor, research
engineer and development
engineer. He lives in Godalm-
ing, Surrey, where he retired
early, at 58 (for health rea-
sons). His wife, Jean, retired
shortly after him, from the
Health Service, where she
served as medical staffing and
personnel officer.

They are immensely proud of
their two sons, Kelvin (who
paraglides or hang-glides al-
most every weekend), and
Adrian, who does post-
doctoral research into ar-
thritis, at Southampton Uni-
versity.

This poem was written a few
days after Jean bought a pair
of tap shoes to resume tap
dancing classes, first begun in
childhood.

Two earlier poems, *Love* and
The Face of Love, have been
published in To Love and Be
Loved.

The Tap Dancer

The tickety tap of dancing feet
The tickey tickety tack.
The tickety tack as she learns the steps of
Tickety trickerty tap.

The years have swept by, the stage long been swept,
The dancing years are gone.
The dancer's steps still haunt her, yet,
She dances on.
Alone.

Yet in the glitter of the eye,
The twinkle of her smile,
We know the dance excites her yet,
And will do.
For a while.

She hears the rhythm in her heart,
And feels another hand.
She must keep up, and keep in time.
The steps have all been planned.

The quickening pace, the ageless grace,
the tickety tickerty tap.
And all the while, she inward smiles.
And waits.
For an answering.
Tap.

R W Kinkaid

Notes

I am 66 years old, a retired local government chief officer, and married to Sheila with a son and two daughters. I also have five grandchildren. I live in a village 12 miles from Stratford-on-Avon having moved from Scotland some 18 years ago.

My hobbies include: voluntary service organisations, walking (30-40 miles weekly), golf, gardening, music, reading and travel, especially France and the USA.

I started writing seriously six years ago at a Creative Writing Class. A good tutor taught me a lot about poetry styles and short story writing. So far I have not tried for publication.

My poetry is inspired mainly by country scenes in nearby fields and hills. I am also aware of social influences. Not disciplined! Could try harder!

Tankas

Grasses greening, spring
Approaching, days lengthening,
Birds nest, small lambs graze,
Frisking and jumping, playful.
Harsh winter is defeated.

Bold green upright stalks
With sun-blessed golden trumpets
Proclaim spring's approach.
No forecast of frost or snow
Can kill anticipation.

Sheep crop the green fields,
Snowy spring lambs, mother ewes.
The fathering rams
Are absent, anonymous;
One more single parent scenario.

She stood there, alone,
Weeping in the winter chill.
Ignoring the rain.
The flowers she had brought
Rested against the cold tombstone.

Charles Girvan

Notes

I am aged 69, married to Sam - a retired gardener - with four daughters and two grandchildren.

My first poem was published in 1947, on the front cover of National Federation of Youth Clubs' magazine as well as inside. The poem was called *When This War is Over - A Call to Youth;* my only published work - 'til now!

I'm inspired by the beauty of nature and a longing for world peace. *Before it is too Late* was written at the time when there was first talk of world disarmament - before the fall of the Berlin Wall - *why* is it taking so long!

My interests are varied; I love music and play the piano, drama - I've done lots of amateur acting and I'm a compulsive knitter! (for Oxfam and Shelter).

Before it is too Late

Disarm you nations - far and wide -
Hold back - it's time to turn the tide,
And stand together side by side
In peace and understanding.
Resources that you waste on war
Could far better be employed to build a world
Where flags of peace fly free - unfurled.
The world is rich - full of wealth which should be shared around.
It's wrong that some should have too much
And some die - starving on the ground.
Let all the hateful barriers fall -
Like the dreaded Berlin Wall -
There let a million flowers grow whose seeds may east or westward blow!
The government of the world should be in the hands of men
Whose concern is its survival - not their own power and gain.
All people of the world - unite.
Together let us all now fight
Starvation - poverty - pollution -
It's vital that we find the solution to the problems that exist
To add to them we must resist.
So let the next war that we wage
Be written down on history's page
As the 'war for peace' which must be won
For all our sakes - yes everyone -
For rich or poor we *all* will perish
Unless this world of ours we cherish.

Hilary Richardson

Forgotten

The simple flowers, draped upon my grave
From somewhere they were lost,
Somewhere along the way,
False in their beauty, they never seem to care,
Of how or why it seems,
Someone is lying there

Eventually they tremble, and fall into the dust,
Wondering why they gave their lives,
As if I'd lost their trust
And now I feel, from somewhere dark,
The closing of a door,
Another life, another place,
And still I die once more.

M L Baxendale

Notes

I was born on October 8th, 1939 at Hertford Hospital and lived at home in Codicote, Herts, until my marriage in 1961. We have lived in Welwyn Garden City, Herts, since then. The Garden City concept was the idea of Ebenezer Howard, a Quaker, who founded Welwyn Garden City in 1920. Industry is separate from the residential areas and the focal point is the garden designed by Louis-de-Soissons.

I dedicate this poem to my father, the late William Gilbert, my mother, Phyllis, and my family everywhere, including Australia and Canada. To the memory of a friend, Shonah McLauchlan, who dedicated her later years helping the homeless and campaigned for world peace. To environmentalists, past and present, who have worked, and who are working with, indigenous peoples, to safeguard their environment, the rainforest and endangered species. Especially to the Vanuatu Protected Areas Initiative, who have helped set up national parks there, and another project is under way, there is now a school education programme.

How Green the Grass

How green the grass, how strong the trees,
The scent of flowers upon the breeze,
A nearby stream, so clean and clear,
How long before it disappears?

When dusk enfolds this wood at night,
I see a barn owl on silent flight,
But chemicals and loss of barns,
Are much too common on most farms.

Rain-forests have a unique part to play,
But more trees are lost each day.
Unique life forms and medicines lost,
Eroded earth, floods, lost lives, a terrible cost.

Teaching children in every land,
So that they will understand,
They must not take the earth for granted,
Wise thoughts, like seeds, are planted.

Susan Groom

Notes

For my father, Vernon, who died 2nd August 1996 and who was the most supportive father anyone could have - commenting only on my life's successes and never on its failures. And for my mother, Dorothy, who keeps me happy by persisting in her belief that I am more clever than reality actually demonstrates!

Robert the Bruce

A man once watched a spider
Spin a web and then
Said 'if at first we don't succeed
We must try again'
I wonder if he asked himself
Whilst reaching this surmise
Just *why* we should emulate
Something that eats dead flies

Roger Knowles

Goodbye My Love

Four autumns and four springs I've known you dear
And hoped that I could always be your friend
But now the time has come for you to leave me here
With memories of you that never end.

They say a man should never really miss
A love denied and never truly had
If that is so, then would they tell me this
Why summer's gone and I am cold and sad.

My love for you I'll try my best to quell
And to my future sorrows readjust
For when you go I'll come and wish you well
Goodbye my love - farewell if go you must

Brian M Furber

King Alfred the Great

Notes

I am ten years old and live in Stafford. I have been writing for about three years now. My inspiration for this poem came from a history book I once came across. It told me that King Alfred the great was one of the most favoured kings throughout the English monarchs.

King Alfred the Great
Came to his fate
In a way which I don't know.

But what I do know is that
He was a bit of a favourite.

Teacher's pet, that's what he was.
Nobody else stood a chance.

The lad used to fight a lot
It was in his blood, they said.
People used to come and complain to the king
Then out of the country they were led.

Alfred had a back-up,
A governess, called Maude
Alfred could do anything and she wouldn't tell,
Even hit her with his sword!

And so at the end of my little tale
I'm disgusted at it all.
No wonder Alfred was a warrior
        He was taught to be when small.

Jenny Hardwick